THE KITE RUNNER

Khaled Hosseini

AUTHORED by Claudine Fernandez
UPDATED AND REVISED by Michelle Rosenberg

COVER DESIGN by Table XI Partners LLC
COVER PHOTO by Olivia Verma and © 2005 GradeSaver, LLC

BOOK DESIGN by Table XI Partners LLC

Published by GradeSaver LLC, www.gradesaver.com

First published in the United States of America by GradeSaver LLC. 2013

ISBN 978-1-60259-389-3

Printed in the United States of America

For other products and additional information please visit
http://www.gradesaver.com

Table of Contents

Table of Contents

Table of Contents

Table of Contents

Teaching Guide - About the Author

Khaled Hosseini was born on March 4, 1965 in Kabul, the capital of Afghanistan, as the oldest of five children. His father worked for the Afghan Foreign Ministry as a diplomat, and his mother was a high school teacher of Farsi and history. When Hosseini was five years old, his family moved from Kabul to Tehran, Iran. They returned to Kabul but eventually sought political asylum in the United States during the Soviet occupation of Afghanistan. The Hosseini family moved to San Jose, California, where Hosseini graduated from high school. He graduated from Santa Clara University with a degree in Biology, and then went on to medical school. Hosseini started writing *The Kite Runner* in 2001 while he was a practicing physician.

Hosseini published *The Kite Runner* in 2003 to critical acclaim. While parts of the novel are based on Hosseini's childhood in the Kabul neighborhood of Wazir Akbar Khan, the novel is fictional. By May 2007, it had been published in thirty-eight countries, but not Afghanistan.

In 2003, while *The Kite Runner* was gaining popularity around the world, Hosseini returned to Afghanistan for the first time in 27 years. He was disturbed to discover just how terrible the situation there had become. Hosseini has stated that a combination of luck and material privilege saved him and his family from suffering under the Soviets and the Taliban, much like his protagonist, Amir. He struggled with his freedom, recalling, "I felt ashamed, like I should have suffered more." Hosseini felt estranged from the devastation in Afghanistan, but his novel brought international attention to the lives of Afghanis.

Hosseini published his second novel, *A Thousand Splendid Suns*, in May 2007 to positive reviews. Unlike *The Kite Runner*, which centers around relationships between men, *A Thousand Splendid Suns* focuses on the stories of women.

Hosseini's devotion to Afghanistan can be seen not only in his writings but also in his advocacy work. He has been a goodwill envoy to the United Nations Refugee Agency (UNHCR) since 2006, and his personal website contains links to many aid organizations that are helping Afghanistan. Interviewers describe Hosseini as a smart, handsome man with a calming air, and Time Magazine called him "almost certainly the most famous Afghan in the world." Khaled Hosseini lives with his wife and two children in Northern California.

Teaching Guide - Study Objectives

If all of the elements of this lesson plan are employed, students will develop the following powers, skills, and understanding:

1. An in-depth understanding of the plot, characters and themes of the novel.
2. An ability to analyze the literary elements of the novel competently.
3. An ability to apply their analysis of the novel to formulate their own arguments and have informed opinions about the novel.
4. An ability to situate the novel within its cultural, social and political contexts.

Teaching Guide - Common Core Standards

- 9 - CCSS.ELA-Literacy.RL.9-10.1 Cite strong and thorough textual evidence to support analysis of what the text says explicitly as well as inferences drawn from the text.

- 9 - CCSS.ELA-Literacy.RL.9-10.2 Determine a theme or central idea of a text and analyze in detail its development over the course of the text, including how it emerges and is shaped and refined by specific details; provide an objective summary of the text.

- 9 - CCSS.ELA-Literacy.RL.9-10.3 Analyze how complex characters (e.g., those with multiple or conflicting motivations) develop over the course of a text, interact with other characters, and advance the plot or develop the theme.

- 9 - CCSS.ELA-Literacy.RL.9-10.5 Analyze how an author's choices concerning how to structure a text, order events within it (e.g., parallel plots), and manipulate time (e.g., pacing, flashbacks) create such effects as mystery, tension, or surprise.

- 9 - CCSS.ELA-Literacy.RL.9-10.6 Analyze a particular point of view or cultural experience reflected in a work of literature from outside the United States, drawing on a wide reading of world literature.

- 9 - CCSS.ELA-Literacy.RL.9-10.6 Analyze a particular point of view or cultural experience reflected in a work of literature from outside the United States, drawing on a wide reading of world literature.

- 9 - CCSS.ELA-Literacy.RL.9-10.6 Analyze a particular point of view or cultural experience reflected in a work of literature from outside the United States, drawing on a wide reading of world literature.

- 9 - CCSS.ELA-Literacy.RL.9-10.7 Analyze the representation of a subject or a key scene in two different artistic mediums, including what is emphasized or absent in each treatment.

Teaching Guide - Introduction to The Kite Runner

The Kite Runner is Khaled Hosseini's first novel. He was a practicing physician until shortly after the book's release and has now devoted himself to being an author and activist. The story of the novel is fictional, but it is rooted in real political and historical events ranging from the last days of the Afghan monarchy in the 1970's to the post-Taliban near-present. It is also based on Hosseini's memories of growing up in the Wazir Akbar Khan section of Kabul and adapting to life in California. In a 2003 interview with *Newsline*, Hosseini specified that the most autobiographical parts of The Kite Runner are those about "the difficult task of assimilating into a new culture." He also revealed, "My father and I did work for a while at the flea market and there really are rows of Afghans working there, some of whom I am related to." Because Hassan did not return to Kabul until 2003, after *The Kite Runner*'s publication, much of his portrayal of Afghanistan after the Soviet takeover is based on research. Hosseini's choice of time period for the book, though corresponding with his own life, also went beyond his personal experiences. He has said that he did not just want to call attention to the devastation in Afghanistan; he set out to remind the world that until the last few decades, before the world's eye was drawn to it by violence, Afghanistan was a generally peaceful nation.

Key Aspects of The Kite Runner

Tone

The novel begins on a reminiscent note as the narrator remembers an event that changed his life. As he begins to convey the story of his childhood, the tone is predominantly one of despair as the characters lead hard lives filled with suffering and misfortune. However, their brave reactions to adversity present feelings of hope and optimism.

Setting

Amir lives in California for most of his adolescent and adult life, after he and Baba move there from Peshawar, Pakistan.

Many scenes from the past are set in Kabul, Afghanistan, where Amir spends most of his childhood.

Point of View

The novel is told in first-person narration, primarily from the point of view of Amir. However, in Chapter 16, the story is told from Rahim Khan's point of view.

Character Development

Amir: The protagonist in the novel and undeniably the character who undergoes the most change and transformation. He changes from a self-centered, immature child to an adult who is able to stand up for himself and what he believes in, protecting fiercely those he loves. For most of the novel, Amir struggles with his guilt but by the end he seems to have reached a kind of reconciliation with himself and a semblance of liberation from that guilt and from his past.

Hassan: Hassan was Amir's closest childhood companion, protector, and loyal servant. He becomes more withdrawn after an incident of sexual assault in his childhood, but his essential qualities do not change much even when he becomes an adult and a father.

Baba: Amir's father, Baba, starts out the novel as a detached parent because Amir is unable to fulfill his expectations of an ideal son. However, the two become closer after they move to America. Later, Amir finds out that Baba had his own guilt to deal with about his affair with Ali's first wife; Baba is actually Hassan's father. Baba tried to compensate for this guilt by doing good works for those in need.

Assef: Assef can be considered the villain or antagonist in this novel. He admires Hitler and espouses his belief in ethnic cleansing and the eradication of the Hazaras, and he rapes Hassan. He later joins the Taliban and is the source of much of the violence and aggression in the novel. However, he is defeated in the end by Sohrab.

Soraya: Soraya is Amir's wife; she plays an important role in Amir's growth and maturity. She is a source of support and solace for Amir during difficult times. She, too, had to struggle with discrimination and being ostracized by her community after eloping with an Afghan man. Soraya is highly principled and answers her calling to become a teacher despite her father's protests.

Rahim Khan: Rahim Khan is Baba's business partner and confidante, but also a father figure to Amir. He was there for Amir, supporting him and encouraging him to pursue his dreams, when Baba was not. He is also the catalyst for Amir's redemption, providing him with a way to be "good again." He also urges Amir to let go of his guilt and to forgive himself.

Themes

Brotherhood

Although they belong to different social classes, Baba treats Ali like a brother. Similarly, Amir and Hassan were more like brothers as opposed to having a master-servant relationship. It is later revealed that Amir and Hassan are actually half-brothers.

Sacrifice

Hassan had to be sacrificed in order for Amir to win Baba's affections. Hassan sacrifices his honor for Amir by taking the blame for stealing the watch. Baba sacrifices his own happiness by moving to America so that Amir can have a better future. Amir sacrifices his safety (and potentially his life) to rescue Sohrab from the clutches of Assef.

Redemption

Characters like Amir and Sanaubar attempt to redeem themselves and make up for past wrongdoings by doing good deeds.

Love

Baba and Ali, and Hassan and Amir, each share a brotherly love and affection. Baba and Amir share familial love, as do Amir and Sohrab and Hassan and Sohrab and Soraya and her parents. Love for family and friends has a redemptive quality, particularly for Amir.

The Effects of Violence

The violence perpetuated by the Taliban on the common people, especially the Hazaras, provides the backdrop for much of the novel. Assef sodomizing Hassan and Assef beating Amir are two of the most violent scenes in the novel, and they have serious emotional repercussions that last well beyond the physical effects of the events themselves.

Symbols

Kite-flying

Winning the kite-flying competition symbolizes a sense of victory and pride for not only Amir and Hassan, but also for Baba. When Amir takes Sohrab kite-flying in the last chapter and runs the kite for him, it symbolizes a form of redemption for his past mistakes.

Books and Stories

In Chapter 12, Soraya is reading *Wuthering Heights*, which shares common themes of sacrifice and love with *The Kite Runner*. In Afghanistan, literacy is tied to one's social status and power. Amir was able to read but Hassan was not, because Amir was privileged enough to go to school. This is why Hassan ensures that Sohrab learns to read, because wishes for Sohrab to have a better life than he did. Ali and Hassan give Amir an illustrated copy of Amir's favorite book, *Shahnamah*, for his birthday, which symbolizes an act of love. Lastly, Rahim Khan recognizes Amir's talent for writing stories, and that recognition helps to catalyze Amir's career as a writer.

Physical Deformities

Hassan's harelip is often pointed out--Baba tries to correct it by offering to pay for plastic surgery, perhaps out of guilt. The scar above Rahim Khan's eye is a reminder of the random acts of violence committed by the Taliban on the general populace. Amir's lip is also cut after Assef beats him, and this could symbolise Amir paying for his wrongdoings.

Dreams

In Chapter 7, Hassan narrates his dream about the monster to Amir. The monster in the dream could symbolize the monster that Amir perceives himself to be when he fails to save Hassan and even frames him for theft. The dream that Amir has of Hassan's murder could be read as a symbol of Amir's guilt that has been haunting him. Amir dreams of Baba merging with him and this could symbolize how alike the two of them are in many ways.

Baba's House

The dilapidated state of Baba's house is reminiscent of the fallen state of Afghanistan since the Russian invasion and the rise of the Taliban. It could also symbolize the fallen status of Baba since he left Kabul. Additionally, the state of the house could represent the status of Amir and Hassan's relationship, which had also degenerated.

Climax

The first climax scene occurs when Hassan is raped by Assef. Amir watches passively and eventually runs away. This sparks off a chain of events leading to Amir feeling guilt-ridden and then framing Hassan for theft, which eventually leads to both Ali and Hassan leaving Baba's house.

The second climax occurs when Amir returns to Kabul to search for Sohrab, which paves the way for his redemption after fighting off Assef and overcoming the obstacles faced when he tries to adopt Sohrab.

Structure

The narrative is a series of flashbacks and flash forwards, rather than having a chronological, linear structure. Moreover, the narrative is also interspersed with dreams and memories, which are manifestations of the narrator's inner landscape. The novel is also fashioned to be a bildungsroman, detailing the personal growth and maturity of the protagonist, Amir.

Teaching Guide - Relationship with Other Books

Khaled Hosseini's *A Thousand Splendid Suns* is a sequel of sorts to *The Kite Runner*. Also set in Afghanistan, the novel explores once again how the political and the personal are intertwined, giving vivid portrayals of the impact of the volatile society on the lives of ordinary people.

Another literary work with a similar setting is *The Bookseller of Kabul* by Asne Selerstad, which details the suffering of the women in a patriarchal family.

The Namesake, by Jhumpa Lahiri, is a narrative of a family who has moved from India to America. The protagonist grows up as the novel progresses, making it akin to the bildungsroman that is *The Kite Runner*.

Teaching Guide - Bringing In Technology

Day 1: Hotseating

Students could record their hotseating sessions in groups before class and upload them to youtube.

Day 1: Hazaras and Pashtuns

Students can use powerpoint or keynote to create and conduct their in-class presentations.

Day 2: Foils

Students can use powerpoint instead of a flipchart.

Day 3: The Taliban in Afghanistan

Use video clips to inform a discussion about Afghanistan's recent history.

Day 4: The Truth Will Set You Free

Students can use google drive or another collaborative editing platform to compose their pieces together.

Day 4: Film Adaptation

Show clips from the film adaptation of the novel.

Day 5: Authorial Intention

Use audio and video clips of interviews with the author.

Teaching Guide - Notes to the Teacher

The thought questions in this lesson plan provide material and ideas that students can use to develop their personal voice and critical thinking skills while writing.

The questions provided for the final paper are most suitable for student essays. Remember that grading an essay should not depend on a simple checklist of required content but the grade given should be a holistic one, bearing in mind the criteria provided in the marking rubric.

Of course, the daily lessons can be expanded into additional days--or consolidated into fewer days--based on the needs of the students and the course.

In terms of content, students might find the violence and sexual abuse a little intense and they might not be used to reading and studying literature that deals with these issues. Make sure to be sensitive in the delivery and discussion of such controversial topics and to always seek students' feedback on how they are coping with the content.

Author of Lesson Plan and Sources

Claudine Fernandez, author of Lesson Plan. Completed on February 08, 2013, copyright held by GradeSaver.

Updated and revised Michelle Rosenberg November 13, 2013. Copyright held by GradeSaver.

"The Economist explains: What is the difference between Sunni and Shia Muslims?." The Economist Explains. 2013-05-28. 2013-08-15. <http://www.economist.com/blogs/economist-explains/2013/05/economist-explains-19>.

Julie Myerson. "Review:The Namesake by Jhumpa Lahiri." The Guardian. 2004-01-16. 2013-08-15. <http://www.theguardian.com/books/2004/jan/17/featuresreviews.guardianreview23>.

Michiko Kakutani. "A Woman's Lot in Kabul, Lower Than a House Cat's." New York Times. 2007-05-29. 2013-08-15. <http://www.nytimes.com/2007/05/29/books/29kaku.html?pagewanted=all&_r=0>.

Tim Judah. "Family at war - with itself." The Guardian. 2003-08-30. 2013-08-15. <http://www.theguardian.com/books/2003/aug/31/travel.features>.

Linda Elder and Richard Paul. "Universal Intellectual Standards." 2013-08-22. <http://www.criticalthinking.org/pages/universal-intellectual-standards/527>.

Linda Elder and Richard Paul. "Universal Intellectual Standards." 2013-08-22. <http://www.criticalthinking.org/pages/universal-intellectual-standards/527>.

"Soviet invasion of Afghanistan." Encyclopædia Britannica. Encyclopædia Britannica Online. Encyclopædia Britannica Inc.. 2013-08-25. 2013-08-22. <http://www.britannica.com/EBchecked/topic/1499983/Soviet-invasion-of-Afghanistan>.

"The Taliban in Afghanistan." Council on Foreign Relations. 2013-08-06. 2013-08-22. <http://www.cfr.org/afghanistan/taliban-afghanistan/p10551>.

Dianne Emmick. "Teaching Materials for The Kite Runner." CNY Reads Committee Syracuse, NY. 2013-08-22. <http://www.onlib.org/cnyreads/0506kite_runner/teaching.htm>.

"The Kite Runner Theme Analysis Lesson." The Khaled Hosseini Foundation. 2013-08-22. <http://www.sos4tkhf.com/downloads/TKR_Theme_Analysis_Lesson.pdf>.

Related Links

http://www.amnestyusa.org/sites/default/files/kiterunnerhigh_0.pdf
The Kite Runner Companion Curriculum A useful site by Amnesty International USA, which provides further teaching and study resources about both the film and the novel.

http://www.youtube.com/watch?v=2czUEHeLQP8
2013 ALA Annual Conference- Interview with Khaled Hosseini An interview with the author hosted by the American Library Association and featured on YouTube.

http://www.npr.org/templates/story/story.php?storyId=4795618
Khaled Hosseini on Fresh Air Terry Gross of WHYY interviews Khaled Hosseini.

Day 1 - Reading Assignment

Read Chapters 1-5

Common Core Objectives

- 1) CCSS.ELA-Literacy.RL.9-10.4 Cite strong and thorough textual evidence to support analysis of what the text says explicitly as well as inferences drawn from the text.

  2) CCSS.ELA-Literacy.RL.9-10.6 Analyze a particular point of view or cultural experience reflected in a work of literature from outside the United States, drawing on a wide reading of world literature.

  3) CCSS.ELA-Literacy.RL.9-10.3 Analyze how complex characters (e.g., those with multiple or conflicting motivations) develop over the course of a text, interact with other characters, and advance the plot or develop the theme.

Note that it is perfectly fine to expand any day's work into two days depending on the characteristics of the class, particularly if the class will engage in all of the suggested classroom exercises and activities and discuss all of the thought questions.

Content Summary for Teachers

Chapter 1: The novel begins with the narrator's recollection of a pivotal moment in his life when he was 12. The recollection is sparked by a call from one of the narrator's friends, Rahim Khan, who requests that the narrator to come and see him in Pakistan. However, it is not as simple as it seems; the narrator views this call as an invitation to atone for his past mistakes. This brief chapter closes with the narrator's memory of his childhood friend Hassan, who is also known as the "harelipped kite runner." The narrator remembers Hassan's haunting words, "For you a thousand times over," as he see a pair of kites above the San Francisco skyline.

Chapter 2: This chapter introduces us to three of the main characters: Amir, the narrator; his childhood playmate Hassan; and Amir's father, Baba. We learn that Amir and Hassan are as close as brothers, but their social status separates them and Hassan is not able to enjoy the privileged life that Amir gets to lead. Yet Hassan remains a loyal companion and servant to Amir. Hassan and his father Ali belong to a minority ethnic group called the Hazaras, while Amir and Baba are Pashtuns, an ethnic group with higher social status. Hassan and his father live in a hut close to Baba's house, and we learn that Hassan's mother left the family soon after Hassan was born. Amir's mother died in childbirth.

Chapter 3: While Baba is known by many for his works in the community and his bravery and strength, Amir reveals to the readers a different side of his father. Baba seems to live by his own moral standards, and does not always abide by the teachings of Islam. Baba tells Amir that there is really only one sin, and that is theft. All other sins are a variation of that. Despite their talks, Amir feels rather detached from his father. He feels that he does not meet Baba's expectations for a son, and so Baba is not proud of him. As a result, Amir craves Baba's attention and is envious of the attention Baba showers on Hassan. The chapter closes with Amir overhearing Baba telling his business partner, Rahim Khan, about Amir not being able to stand up for himself. Amir then takes it out on Hassan the following morning.

Chapter 4: Although Baba seems to treat Ali like a brother, Amir notices astutely that Baba never refers to Ali as his friend; ultimately, the reality is that Ali is Baba's servant. Amir applies this to his own relationship with Hassan. Amir asserts and abuses his superiority over Hassan, at times tricking Hassan by telling him incorrect definitions for certain words. Ironically, it is through Amir's trickery that he discovers his talent for storytelling; he changes the plot of a story that he is reading to Hassan, much to Hassan's delight. While Rahim Khan and Hassan encourage Amir's penchant for storytelling, Baba does not seem to care. The chapter ends at the moment that Amir tells us "Afghanistan changed forever," but we do not find out what the event was.

Chapter 5:

For Hassan and Amir, gunfire marks the beginning of Daoud Khan's bloodless coup, which ends Afghanistan's monarchy in 1973. The next morning, as Hassan and Amir try to go about their normal lives, Hassan is taunted by Assef, the neighborhood bully. Assef admires Hitler's ethnic cleansing and believes that the same should be done with the Hazaras in Afghanistan. Assef also taunts Amir for treating a Hazara as a friend; Amir nearly blurts out that Hassan is actually his servant, and not his friend, but he stops himself. Assef tries to hit Amir, but Hassan fires a slingshot at him. In response, Assef threatens Amir and Hassan, vowing that he will get his revenge soon.

The narrative then shifts to the following winter, when Baba offers to pay for Hassan's cleft lip surgery as a birthday gift. After the successful surgery, Hassan smiles with gratitude and happiness, but the narrator reveals to us rather forebodingly that the following winter, Hassan stopped smiling.

Thought Questions (students consider while they read)

1. What is the relationship between the Hazaras and the Pashtuns in Afghanistan?
2. How does Amir portray Baba in these chapters?

3. How does Assef's behavior reveal aspects of other characters in Chapter 5?
4. Describe Amir and Hassan's relationship in this section.
5. How did Amir feel about Hassan getting the cleft lip surgery? Why is this important?

Vocabulary (in order of appearance)

Chapter 1, pg. 2:

- harelip: derogatory term for a birth defect where the upper lip has a cleft in it

Chapter 2, pg. 8:

- unscrupulous: without any morals

Chapter 2, pg. 10:

- obstetricians: medical specialists who deal with childbirth
- anesthesiologists: trained medical physicians who administer drugs to put a patient to sleep or to numb sensations, usually before surgical operations

Chapter 2, pg. 14:

- caracul hat: a hat made of the skin of a Persian lamb

Chapter 2, pg. 15:

- mullah: a revered person who teaches and propagates the Islamic faith

Chapter 2, pg. 17:

- tittering: stifling giggles

Chapter 2, pg. 21:

- valiant: brave

Chapter 4, pg. 24:

- hashish: dried parts of a plant which people smoke to get a feeling of intoxication

Chapter 4, pg. 27:

- lumbered: moved heavily

Chapter 4, pg. 31:

- feigned: fake

Chapter 4, page 32:

- hunkered: bent over

Chapter 5, page 15:

- staccato: a musical term, associated with short and abrupt sounds

Chapter 5, page 37:

- coup: an overthrow of the government or those in power

Chapter 5, page 38:

- pummeled: beat several times with one's fists
- badgering: pestering in an annoying and constant manner

Chapter 5, pg. 40:

- grandiose: overly large or exaggerated

Chapter 5, pg. 42:

- hierarchy: a social structure defining who has power and status

Additional Homework

1. Glossary of terms: There are many colloquialisms and foreign words used, which have been italicized in the text. Students could work in groups or individually to pick out these italicized words from every chapter and create a glossary. This could be an ongoing assignment which lasts throughout the unit.

Day 1 - Discussion of Thought Questions

1. What is the relationship between the Hazaras and the Pashtuns in Afghanistan?

   Time: 5-10 mins

   Discussion:

   The Pashtuns and the Hazaras are two ethnic groups in Afghanistan. The Hazaras make up a smaller proportion of the population while the Pashtuns are the dominant group. Most Hazaras are Shi'a Muslims, while most Pashtuns are Sunni Muslims. There is significant conflict between the Pashtuns and the Hazaras in Afghanistan, with the Hazaras often persecuted by the Pashtun majority.

   The class can also discuss the following context about Sunni and Shi'a Islam: Both religious groups believe in the God of the Bible and the Koran, but the Sunnis follow only the teachings of the Prophet Muhammad, while the Shia see their Ayatollahs (religious leaders) as reflections of God. The schism first happened with a dispute in the 7th century over

2. How does Amir portray Baba in these chapters?

   Time: 5 mins

   Discussion: Baba is portrayed as an alpha-male figure with traditionally masculine strengths and ideals. We also learn that he is very generous, having built an orphanage and taking good care of Ali and Hassan, both of whom he shares a close relationship with. We also learn that he is not much of a father figure to Amir whom he remains detached from because Amir does not match up to his ideals.

3. How does Assef's behavior reveal aspects of other characters in Chapter 5?

Time: 5 mins

Discussion: Assef is portrayed as a ruffian and a bully. It is significant that his bullying of the two boys allows us to form our own impressions about Hassan and Amir's characters respectively. Readers are likely to see Hassan as a kind of protector and defender of Amir, while Amir appears cowardly when he does not dare to stand up to Assef on behalf of Hassan.

4. Describe Amir and Hassan's relationship in this section.

   Time: 10 mins

   Discussion: While Amir and Hassan seem to have a very close childhood friendship and brotherhood, their relationship is indeed quite complex. No matter how much Amir enjoys Hassan's comforting companionship, he is unable to forget the fact that Hassan is his servant. Despite Hassan's loyalty and sincerity, Amir is constantly trying to assert and even abuse his superiority over Hassan. Hassan. on the other hand, knows his place in the society and he accepts Amir's treatment without complaint. In fact, he seems to be extremely content in his role as Amir's servant.

5. How did Amir feel about Hassan getting the cleft lip surgery? Why is this important?

   Time: 5 mins

   Discussion: Amir feels jealous about his father's sympathy and kindness toward Hassan. Amir begins to wish that he too had a deformity which would invite the same kind of sympathy. Such episodes of jealousy have been accumulating over the years, and they will culminate in a traumatic scene later on in the novel. Students might be able to sympathize with Amir's feelings of jealousy and his desire to be treated more affectionately and sympathetically by Baba.

Day 1 - Short Answer Quiz

1. What did Hassan's mother do shortly after Hassan was born?

2. What does Baba tell Amir about sin?

3. How does Rahim Khan defend Amir in response to Baba's criticisms?

4. What does Assef believe about the Hazaras?

5. How does Amir find out the moment at which "Afghanistan had changed forever"?

6. Why do the older children make fun of Ali when they see him on the streets?

7. Why does Amir put his arm around Hassan in the movie theater?

8. Why does Amir bring up the topic of drinking alcohol to Baba?

9. How did Amir's grandfather die?

10. Why does Amir cry at the Buzkashi tournament that he attends with Baba?

Short Answer Quiz Key

1. She had left the family and eloped.
2. He tells Amir that all sins are actually just different types of theft.
3. Rahim Khan accuses Baba of being self-centered and expecting Amir to follow in his footsteps. Khan also advises Baba not to oversimplify his understanding of Amir, and to allow Amir to find his own way.
4. He believes that they are an inferior race that needs to be wiped out of Afghanistan in order for the nation to be pure.
5. He hears roaring gunshots, which he later learns marked the beginning of political unrest in Afghanistan.
6. Ali had polio earlier in life, which caused him to have a limp, leading the older children to call him names like "Babalu" and "flat-nosed Babalu."
7. Amir was comforting Hassan, who was upset because a soldier had insulted his mother.
8. A Mullah in Amir's school teaches him that drinking is a sin. When Baba is drinking in his study one day, Amir decides that it is an opportune time to broach the topic.
9. He was stabbed in the throat when he confronted a thief who had walked into his house.
10. Amir witnesses a horrific and gruesome scene of a horseman falling out of his saddle and being trampled by his horse.

Day 1 - Crossword Puzzle

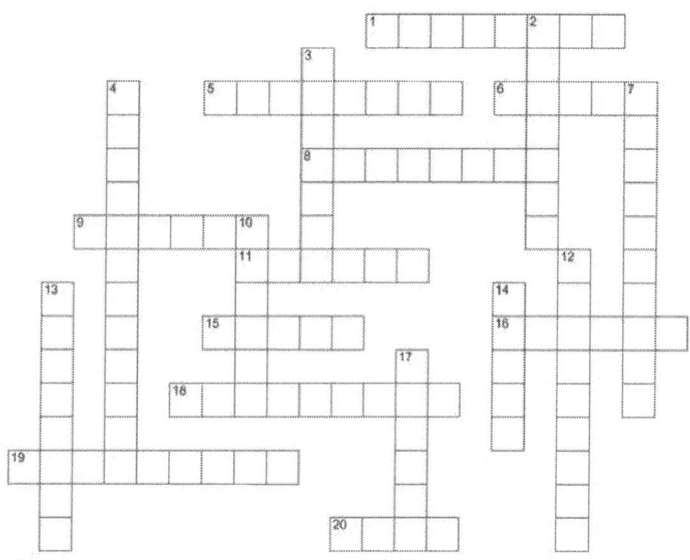

ACROSS

1. Afghanistan's national sport
5. rule by a single person in power, usually a king or queen
6. Rahim Khan encouraged Amir to do this
8. an offensive description of a person who behaves in a mentally deficient way
9. a revered person who teaches and propagates the Islamic faith
11. to attack suddenly
15. the city in Afghanistan that Amir and Hassan grew up in
16. the leader that Assef admired
18. the name of Hassan's favorite book
19. the weapon that Hassan threatened to attack Assef with
20. overthrowing of the government or those in power

DOWN

2. Baba's birthday gift to Hassan
3. brave
4. the removal of the foreskin of a penis
7. affection
10. Hassan's ethnic group
12. stifling giggles
13. Afghanistan became this when its monarchy was overthrown
14. a piece
17. the derogatory nickname given to Ali by some of the older children in the neighborhood

Crossword Puzzle Answer Key

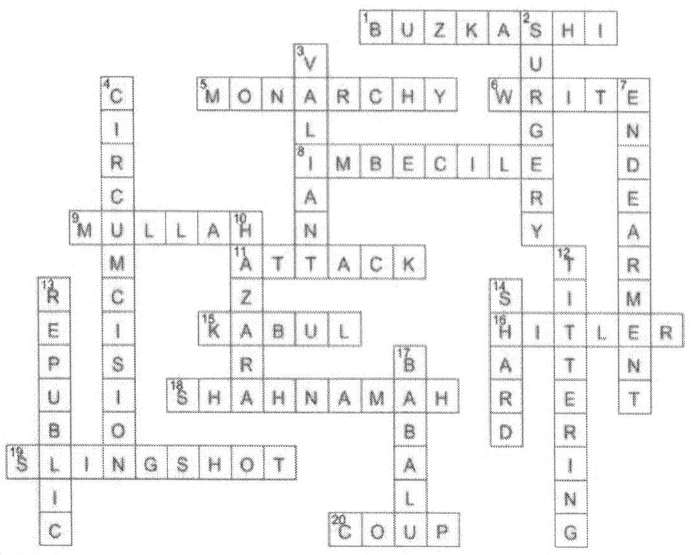

ACROSS

1. Afghanistan's national sport
5. rule by a single person in power, usually a king or queen
6. Rahim Khan encouraged Amir to do this
8. an offensive description of a person who behaves in a mentally deficient way
9. a revered person who teaches and propagates the Islamic faith
11. to attack suddenly
15. the city in Afghanistan that Amir and Hassan grew up in
16. the leader that Assef admired
18. the name of Hassan's favorite book
19. the weapon that Hassan threatened to attack Assef with
20. overthrowing of the government or those in power

DOWN

2. Baba's birthday gift to Hassan
3. brave
4. the removal of the foreskin of a penis
7. affection
10. Hassan's ethnic group
12. stifling giggles
13. Afghanistan became this when its monarchy was overthrown
14. a piece
17. the derogatory nickname given to Ali by some of the older children in the neighborhood

Day 1 - Vocabulary Quiz

Terms		Answers
1. ____	obstetricians	A. dried parts of a plant which people smoke to get a feeling of intoxication
2. ____	caracul hat	B. bent over
3. ____	badgering	C. moved heavily
4. ____	harelip	D. to attack suddenly
5. ____	hashish	E. trained medical physicians who administer drugs to put a patient to sleep or to numb sensations, usually before surgical operations
6. ____	hierarchy	F. a hat made of the skin of a Persian lamb
7. ____	hunkered	G. without any morals
8. ____	lumbered	H. pestering in an annoying and constant manner
9. ____	ambush	I. brave
10. ____	tittering	J. stifling giggles
11. ____	grandiose	K. derogatory term for a birth defect where the upper lip has a cleft in it
12. ____	pummeled	L. overly large and exaggerated
13. ____	imbecile	M. an offensive description of a person who behaves in a mentally deficient way
14. ____	valiant	N. a musical term, associated with short and abrupt sounds
15. ____	coup	O. a social structure defining who has power and status
16. ____	unscrupulous	P. medical specialists who deal with childbirth
17. ____	staccato	Q. an overthrow of the government or those in power
18. ____	anesthesiologists	R. beat several times with one's fists

Vocabulary Quiz Answer Key

1. P
2. F
3. H
4. K
5. A
6. O
7. B
8. C
9. D
10. J
11. L
12. R
13. M
14. I
15. Q
16. G
17. N
18. E

Day 1 - Classroom Activities

1. Hotseating

Kind of Activity: Role Play
Objective: Students will gain a more in-depth understanding of the characters in the novel.
Common Core State Standards: CCSS.ELA-Literacy.RL.9-10.1, CCSS.ELA-Literacy.RL.9-10.3
Time: 30-45 mins

Structure:

The teacher picks three representatives from the class to represent these three characters:

1) Amir

2) Baba

3) Hassan

These three representatives will be placed on a "hot seat" in front of the rest of the class, who will be audience members. The audience members will be tasked with asking questions of the characters based on today's reading. The characters have to respond based on textual evidence and their own extrapolations. At any time, students from the audience can step in to suggest more accurate answers to the students in the hot seat, if they are giving false or inaccurate answers. This activity can also be conducted in small groups of 3 or 4, where the students take turns sitting in the hot seat in front of a smaller audience of questioners. If the activity is done in groups, convene after each hot seat session to discuss what each group asked, how the characters answered, and what if any differences came up across the groups.

Ideans for Differentiated Instruction:

-Choose students who are more comfortable with performing (and particularly with improvisation) to be in the hot seat, while students who are less comfortable can remain in the audience of questioners.

-Encourage all audience members to come up with questions, even if they do not necessarily ask them during the activity.

-If students are struggling to come up with questions for the hot seaters, point them toward passages that might help to generate questions or discussion points.

Assessment Ideas:

-After the activity, students could submit a journal entry based on one of the characters who have been in the "hot seat" based on both the questions and answers from the activity, and any others that the student might devise.

-If you conduct the activity in small groups, have each group designate a scribe and turn in notes from the activity to the instructor.

2. Hazaras and Pashtuns

Kind of Activity: Research
Objective: Students should gain a greater understanding of the cultural, social and religious differences of these two ethnic groups in Afghanistan
Common Core State Standards: CCSS.ELA-Literacy.RL.9-10.6
Time: 30 mins

Structure:

Before this activity, have the students conduct research on the two major ethnic groups in Afghanistan: the Hazaras and the Pashtuns. They should pay particular attention to the differences (both actual and perceived) between these two groups, including differences of social class, ethnic origins, religious beliefs, and cultural practices. Divide the class into groups and assign each group a different area of focus.

Have each group give a brief presentation to the class about the results of their research. Then lead a class discussion about the ethnic conflict in Afghanistan, informed by the student presentations as well as clips from news programs, excerpts from articles, and other sources.

Ideans for Differentiated Instruction:

-Assign students to groups according to complementary skill sets and strengths, and encourage them to take on roles that are appropriate for their strengths.

-Allow students to use powerpoint or keynote, show video clips, or provide handouts as appropriate.

Assessment Ideas:

-At the end of the activity, have students complete a peer evaluation form, either evaluating the contributions of their group members or evaluating the presentations based on the content and delivery of the presentation.

-Assess the student presentations themselves, including any audiovisual materials or handouts provided by the student groups.

Day 2 - Reading Assignment

Read Chapters 6-10.

Common Core Objectives

- 1)CCSS.ELA-Literacy.RL.9-10.1 Cite strong and thorough textual evidence to support analysis of what the text says explicitly as well as inferences drawn from the text.

  2)CCSS.ELA-Literacy.RL.9-10.3 Analyze how complex characters (e.g., those with multiple or conflicting motivations) develop over the course of a text, interact with other characters, and advance the plot or develop the theme.

  3)CCSS.ELA-Literacy.RL.9-10.6 Analyze a particular point of view or cultural experience reflected in a work of literature from outside the United States, drawing on a wide reading of world literature.

Note that it is perfectly fine to expand any day's work into two days depending on the characteristics of the class, particularly if the class will engage in all of the suggested classroom exercises and activities and discuss all of the thought questions.

Content Summary for Teachers

Chapter 6:

The chapter opens at the start of winter, which was always Amir's favorite season. He speaks fondly of one of Kabul's famous winter traditions: the kite-fighting tournament. Flying kites is one of the few activities that brings Amir and Baba closer.

When kites fall out of the sky in the tournament, especially the last kite to fall, those not flying their own kites chase them and try to catch them--these people are called "kite runners." Hassan is an exceptionally good kite runner.

In the winter of 1975, Amir watches Hassan run his last kite. The day before the tournament, Baba suggests that Amir might be able to win this year, and both Hassan and Amir are anxious to please Baba by fulfilling his prediction. That night, the family discusses the fact that Afghanistan might get television under Daoud Khan, and Amir promises to buy Hassan a television one day.

Chapter 7:

Amir wins the tournament, but he does not take sole credit and includes Hassan in his victory. After winning, Amir witnesses Baba's pride on his face and describes it as the 'single greatest moment' of his life thus far. Hassan then swiftly volunteers to run the blue kite that Amir had taken down, saying, 'for you a thousand times over!'

Amir looks for Hassan in the bazaar and finds him trapped in an alleyway with Assef and two other bullies. Assef is trying to exact his revenge on Hassan for hitting him with a slingshot. Assef demands that Hassan hand over the blue kite to him, but out of loyalty to Amir, Hassan refuses.

Amir remembers that he and Hassan are essentially brothers, having fed from the same breast. He also remembers a fortune teller warning Hassan of something disastrous in his future. These memories interrupt the narrative, but it then shifts back to the present, where Assef is about to rape Hassan while his two accomplices hold Hassan down. Amir watches this horrific scene without a word until he cannot bear to watch anymore, and runs away. He admits to himself that he is a coward, but rationalizes that Hassan has to be sacrificed in order for Amir to have all of Baba's affections. Amir runs home to Baba's arms, where he temporarily forgets what he has done.

Chapter 8:

Ali notices a visible change in Hassan's behavior, but Amir shrugs it off when asked about it. Amir asks Baba to take him on a trip to Jalalabad, attempting to spend quality time with him. But Amir is disappointed when Baba suggests inviting Hassan, and then invites another two dozen people along. Meanwhile, there is a growing distance between Hassan and Amir. Although Hassan is determined to bridge the gap between them, Amir keeps rejecting him because he is still tormented by guilt. It is this same guilt that prompts him to ask Baba if he has ever considered hiring new servants. Baba reacts with fury and says that he would never betray Ali in that way. Amir and Hassan go up the hill together, and Amir starts hitting Hassan with a pomegranate, hoping that Hassan will hit him back and alleviate his guilt. Hassan does not fight back, and instead takes a pomegranate and hits his own head before walking away.

The chapter ends with Amir turning thirteen. Amir alienates himself from the guests at his party, but has a surprisingly heartwarming conversation with Rahim Khan. Khan also gives him a leather-bound book in which to write his stories. Amidst the fireworks, Amir spots Hassan serving drinks to Assef and his accomplice, Wali. Assef continues to bully Hassan with pleasure. The sight makes Amir extremely uncomfortable.

Chapter 9: Baba gives Amir two presents for his birthday: a bicycle and a watch. Yet instead of feeling gratitude, Amir knows that he and Baba are still distant and nothing has changed about their relationship. Amir then decides to frame Hassan for theft of his watch so that Baba will dismiss him. He tries to justify it by reasoning that it would also make Hassan's life easier. But when Baba confronts Hassan about stealing the watch, Hassan admits to it without protest, sacrificing himself again for Amir. Baba decides to forgive Hassan, which shocks Amir. Ali nevertheless decides to leave the household with Hassan, to Baba's dismay. Although Amir feels guilty, he does nothing to rectify the situation.

Chapter 10: Five years later, Baba and Amir leave for Pakistan, as life in Afghanistan has become too unstable. When the truck carrying them stops at a checkpoint, a Russian soldier announces that he wants half an hour with an Afghan woman at the back of the truck in order to let them pass the checkpoint. Baba tries to defend the woman. When Amir tries to stop his father out of fear, Baba is ashamed at Amir's cowardice. Also on the truck are Kamal, one of Assef's good friends and accomplices, and Kamal's father. When Kamal dies, poisoned by the truck's fumes, his father commits suicide out of grief. Amir is clearly disturbed by the tragedy.

Thought Questions (students consider while they read)

1. Compare and contrast Hassan and Amir.
2. In Chapter 6 of this section, there is a lot of description about kite-flying and kite-fighting. How are kite-flying and kite-fighting used as metaphors here?
3. What do you think is the significance of the two memories that Amir describes in Chapter 7?
4. Amir is guilt-ridden after passively watching Hassan be assaulted, and then running away. How is the theme of guilt manifested in this section?
5. Discuss the significance of Kamal's violation and eventual death, as it relates to Amir.

Vocabulary (in order of appearance)

Chapter 6, pg. 49:

- epilepsy: a disorder of the nervous system that causes seizures

Chapter 6, pg. 51:

- hovel: a small shelter that sometimes takes the form of a hut or a shed

Chapter 6, pg. 53:

- rutted: characterized by grooves
- wheezing: struggling to breathe, producing a whistling sound

Chapter 6, pg. 54:

- indignation: anger borne out of a sense of injustice

Chapter 6, pg. 55:

- footfalls: footsteps

Chapter 6, pg. 57:

- panjpar: an Afghani card game

Chapter 7, pg. 61:

- austere: severe in appearance
- morose: gloomy

Chapter 7, pg. 63:

- besting: defeating

Chapter 7, pg. 67:

- unabashedly: without any shame or embarrassment

Chapter 7, pg. 68:

- scuttled: ran quickly

Chapter 7, pg. 78:

- guileless: innocent, naive

Chapter 8, pg. 81:

- scuffle: struggle or fight

Chapter 8, pg. 88:

- periphery: edge

Chapter 8, pg. 91:

- harried: troubled
- wince: a facial expression which shows a revulsion to something

Chapter 8, pg. 92:

- pelted: attacked in an unrelenting manner

Chapter 8, pg 93:

- trudged: walked with difficulty because of fatigue

Chapter 8, pg. 93:

- interlude: interval or a transitory time

Chapter 8, pg. 94:

- teeming: brimming

Chapter 8, pg. 97:

- squirmed: wriggled

Chapter 9, pg. 105:

- raspy: having a rough, harsh sound

Chapter 9, pg. 107:

- searing: burning and leaving a mark

Chapter 10, pg. 111:

- tarpaulin: a waterproof protective covering made of materials such as canvas

Additional Homework

1. Ask students to diagram the changes in tone and mood in this section and analyze how and why the tone changes so abruptly, through close analysis of the textual features.

Day 2 - Discussion of Thought Questions

1. Compare and contrast Hassan and Amir.

   Time: 10 mins

   Discussion: Both Hassan and Amir had no knowledge of their mother and were brought up by their fathers. However, Hassan seems to be a more simple and pure character who has a childlike innocence. Amir, on the other hand, does not always have the purest of intentions and thoughts. Because the readers are privy to Amir's thoughts, we know that he is a three-dimensional character whose thoughts are not all good and generous. He believes he is entitled to the social superiority that he has over Hassan. But while Amir might have material privileges and an education, Hassan is rich because he has the love of his father, which Amir lacks. Hassan also appears to be more religious than Amir, who is somewhat agnostic.

2. In Chapter 6 of this section, there is a lot of description about kite-flying and kite-fighting. How are kite-flying and kite-fighting used as metaphors here?

   Time: 10 mins

   Discussion: Just as kite-fighting requires a main kite-fighter and an assistant, the real-life dynamics of Hassan and Amir's relationship play out in this way, with Amir taking center stage and Hassan always playing the supporting role. A kite-fighter also needs a good strategy, determination, and faith in order to win. These are qualities which are needed in real life as well, especially when one is living in a politically unstable setting like Afghanistan. Kite-fighting also has its own set of rules, just like the social and moral codes which govern our lives.

3. What do you think is the significance of the two memories that Amir describes in Chapter 7?

Time: 10 mins

Discussion: The first memory (Ali telling him that he and Hassan fed from the same breast) is significant because it foreshadows the revelation later in the text that they are half-brothers. This memory also makes Amir's actions seem more morally reprehensible, as the two are not just master and servant, but closer to brothers. The second memory is significant because the ominous and mysterious predictions of the fortune-teller may finally be coming true. The second memory reminds us that Hassan is not supposed to lead an easy life.

4. Amir is guilt-ridden after passively watching Hassan be assaulted, and then running away. How is the theme of guilt manifested in this section?

   Time: 10 mins

   Discussion: Amir's guilt is depicted in several ways. First of all, he is unable to face Hassan and tries to have minimal contact with him, which strains their relationship. When Hassan tries to mend the ties between them, Amir becomes more overwhelmed with guilt and tries to provoke a violent reaction from Hassan, albeit unsuccessfully. The guilt then becomes a catalyst for Amir to frame Hassan for theft, because he can no longer bear living in the same house with him. Hassan is a constant reminder of Amir's moral indiscretions, and Amir destroys their relationship rather than dealing with his feelings.

5. Discuss the significance of Kamal's violation and eventual death, as it relates to Amir.

   Time: 5 mins

   Discussion: When the readers first hear of this incident, they might have the impression that it is rather commonplace in Afghanistan and that children are vulnerable to such violence and abuse. It is difficult to sympathize with with Kamal himself, as he was an accomplice to Hassan's rape, but it is similarly hard not to sympathize with the boy's father, who dies of grief shortly after Kamal's death. The reader may even feel that the death is too tragic a price to pay for what Kamal did.

Day 2 - Short Answer Quiz

1. Why did Baba have a hard time adjusting to life in America?

2. What was the first memory that Amir had while he was watching Hassan's assaul?

3. How did Hassan rationalize running away from the scene of the rape?

4. Why did Hassan not dispute the allegation that he had stolen Amir's watch?

5. What does Amir say is the single greatest moment of his life?

6. Why did Amir pray before the kite tournament?

7. Why does Hassan refuse to give the kite to Assef?

8. Why does Baba react angrily when Amir suggests getting new servants?

9. Why did Amir feel unworthy of Ali and Hassan's kindness?

10. Why did Baba attempt to stand up for the woman in the truck on the way to Pakistan?

Short Answer Quiz Key

1. He did not have riches or a high status in America and in fact, was struggling to make ends meet. This was unlike his life in Afghanistan.
2. He remembered Rahim Khan telling him that both Hassan and Amir had fed from the same breast.
3. He tried to justify it by thinking of Hassan as the sacrificial lamb that had to be slain on order for Amir to get Baba's attention and affection.
4. Amir thinks that Hassan had admitted to a wrongdoing which he did not commit in order for Amir not to be implicated. If Hassan were to deny the theft, Baba might find out that Amir had lied and would never have forgiven Amir. Hassan was thus trying to save Amir.
5. Seeing the pride on Baba's face after winning the kite tournament.
6. He was feeling anxious and he said a prayer to calm himself down.
7. Out of loyalty to Amir.
8. Baba becomes angry because he has always treated Ali and Hassan like family, and would never think of replacing them.
9. They had given him the most thoughtful present for his birthday even though they could barely afford it, and they had always been loyal and respectful towards him. However, Amir had betrayed Hassan a number of times at this point, and felt unworthy of loyalty or kindness.
10. The woman was being harassed by a Russian official at the border checkpoint. Baba felt that a strong injustice had been committed and he wanted to reprimand the official for it.

Day 2 - Crossword Puzzle

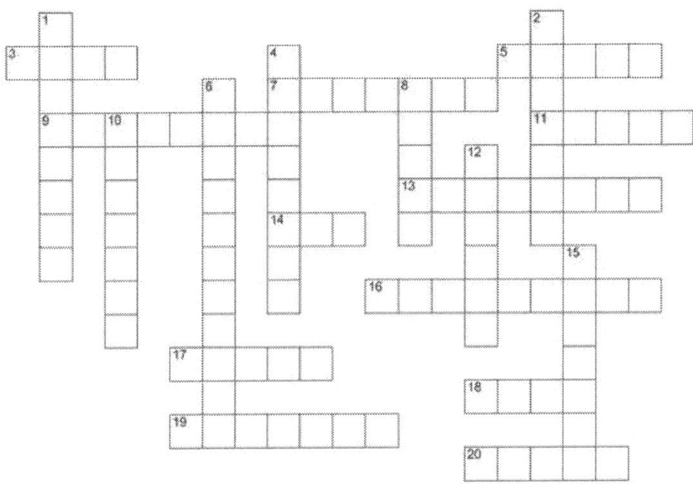

ACROSS

3. the color of the kite which Hassan runs after for Amir
5. the item which Hassan was framed for stealing
7. a black mineral substance used to cement the surface of pavements
9. Rahim Khan's birthday gift to Amir
11. hoarse quality of voice
13. seizures caused by a disorder of the nervous system in the body
14. the number of gifts which Baba gives to Amir for his birthday
16. interval or a transitory time
17. the name of the boy who is poisoned by gas fumes from the truck
18. the location of the monster in Hassan's dream
19. burning and leaving a mark
20. a small shelter that sometimes takes the form of a hut or a shed

DOWN

1. withdrew
2. troubled
4. the place where Baba and Hassan temporarily escape to in a truck
6. the fruit which Hassan pelts his own head with
8. the place where Hassan was being raped
10. walked with difficulty because of fatigue
12. the season when the kite fighting tournament was held
15. appearance of severity of solemnity

Crossword Puzzle Answer Key

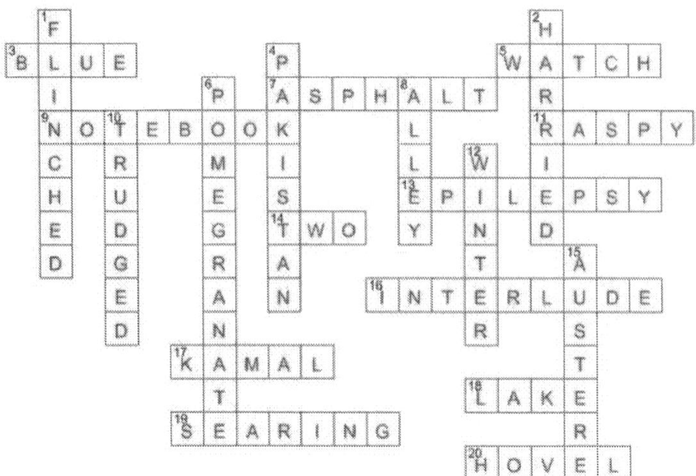

ACROSS

3. the color of the kite which Hassan runs after for Amir
5. the item which Hassan was framed for stealing
7. a black mineral substance used to cement the surface of pavements
9. Rahim Khan's birthday gift to Amir
11. hoarse quality of voice
13. seizures caused by a disorder of the nervous system in the body
14. the number of gifts which Baba gives to Amir for his birthday
16. interval or a transitory time
17. the name of the boy who is poisoned by gas fumes from the truck
18. the location of the monster in Hassan's dream
19. burning and leaving a mark
20. a small shelter that sometimes takes the form of a hut or a shed

DOWN

1. withdrew
2. troubled
4. the place where Baba and Hassan temporarily escape to in a truck
6. the fruit which Hassan pelts his own head with
8. the place where Hassan was being raped
10. walked with difficulty because of fatigue
12. the season when the kite fighting tournament was held
15. appearance of severity of solemnity

Day 2 - Vocabulary Quiz

Terms

1. ____ epilepsy
2. ____ hovel
3. ____ rutted
4. ____ wheezing
5. ____ indignation
6. ____ footfalls
7. ____ panjpar
8. ____ austere
9. ____ morose
10. ____ besting
11. ____ unabashedly
12. ____ scuttled
13. ____ harried
14. ____ trudged
15. ____ teeming
16. ____ squirmed
17. ____ raspy
18. ____ searing
19. ____ tarpaulin

Answers

A. a small shelter that sometimes takes the form of a hut or a shed
B. severe in appearance
C. brimming
D. struggling to breathe, producing a whistling sound
E. troubled
F. an Afghani card game
G. gloomy
H. wriggled
I. walked with difficulty because of fatigue
J. ran quickly
K. characterized by grooves
L. having a rough, harsh sound
M. burning and leaving a mark
N. anger borne out of a sense of injustice
O. defeating
P. without any shame or embarrassment
Q. a waterproof protective covering made of materials such as canvas
R. footsteps
S. seizures caused by a disorder of the nervous system in the body

Vocabulary Quiz Answer Key

1. S
2. A
3. K
4. D
5. N
6. R
7. F
8. B
9. G
10. O
11. P
12. J
13. E
14. I
15. C
16. H
17. L
18. M
19. Q

Day 2 - Classroom Activities

1. Foils

Kind of Activity: Group Work
Objective: Students will understand the literary concept of a foil.
Common Core State Standards: CCSS.ELA-Literacy.RL.9-10.1, CCSS.ELA-Literacy.RL.9-10.3
Time: 20-30 mins

Structure:

This task should be completed in groups of 3-4. Each group is given a flip-chart which is divided vertically into two sides, one labeled "Hassan" and one labeled "Amir."

In their groups, students should discuss the differences between the two characters, listing these qualities on the corresponding side of the flip-chart. Emphasize that although the groups might discuss similarities between the characters as well, only contrasting qualities should be recorded in the chart.

Students should be able to substantiate these qualities using specific examples from the text, making notes about textual references separately from the chart itself.

After about 15 minutes, have the class re-convene. Instruct each group to present their charts to the rest of the class, and provide time for students to ask questions and discuss any differences in their findings. After the presentation, explain the literary term "foil" and show how Amir and Hassan can be considered foils to one another based on the exercises the class has just completed.

Ideans for Differentiated Instruction:

Provide scaffolding questions, or identify particularly relevant passages, for students who are struggling.

Assign students different roles within their groups, according to their strengths (e.g. stronger note-takers might serve as scribes, those comfortable with public speaking might present the group's chart to the class).

Assessment Ideas:

-Have students submit their charts and notes to the instructor for evaluation.

-Assess students' presentations and responses to questions in class, particularly their ability to support and defend their ideas with textual evidence.

2. Debate

Kind of Activity: Classwide Discussion
Objective: Students should be able to present a cogent and coherent argument based on sound textual analysis.
Common Core State Standards: CCSS.ELA-Literacy.RL.9-10.1, CCSS.ELA-Literacy.RL.9-10.6
Time: 30-40 mins

Structure:

In this debate activity, several students will be picked from the class as debaters and divided into two groups, with one group opposing the following statement and the other defending it:

"There is no justifiable reason for Amir to have betrayed Hassan."

The debaters should prepare beforehand, developing arguments based on textual evidence and any research that might be relevant. Students will be given three minutes each to present their case, as well as time for questions and final arguments.

The remaining students will serve as an audience and as members of the jury, who will determine which group wins. After the debate is over, the class should discuss the process and what they learned both during their research and preparation, and during the exercise itself.

Ideans for Differentiated Instruction:

-Select students who are comfortable with public speaking to serve as debaters. Other students on each debate team might do research or collect textual evidence.

-Provide resources for students who have difficulty developing their speeches and debating questions.

Assessment Ideas:

-Students could post on an online forum three key takeaways they had from the debate. The instructor can then evaluate the posts based on demonstrated understanding of the ideas brought forth in the debate, the depth of thought, and clarity in the presentation of these takeaways.

-The instructor can evaluate the debate performance itself, and the quality of the questions asked by the audience/jury.

Day 3 - Reading Assignment

Read Chapters 11-15.

Common Core Objectives

- 1) CCSS.ELA-Literacy.RL.9-10.1 Cite strong and thorough textual evidence to support analysis of what the text says explicitly as well as inferences drawn from the text.

  2) CCSS.ELA-Literacy.RL.9-10.2 Determine a theme or central idea of a text and analyze in detail its development over the course of the text, including how it emerges and is shaped and refined by specific details; provide an objective summary of the text

  3) CCSS.ELA-Literacy.RL.9-10.3 Analyze how complex characters (e.g., those with multiple or conflicting motivations) develop over the course of a text, interact with other characters, and advance the plot or develop the theme

  4) CCSS.ELA-Literacy.RL.9-10.6 Analyze a particular point of view or cultural experience reflected in a work of literature from outside the United States, drawing on a wide reading of world literature.

Note that it is perfectly fine to expand any day's work into two days depending on the characteristics of the class, particularly if the class will engage in all of the suggested classroom exercises and activities and discuss all of the thought questions.

Content Summary for Teachers

Chapter 11: Baba and Amir have moved to Fremont, California. While Baba has some difficulty adapting to life in America, Amir sees it as a place where he can start afresh and forget about his guilt and about Hassan. Amir graduates from high school and plans to major in Creative Writing at a junior college. Baba buys a Volkswagen bus, which they both drive to sell used goods at the San Jose flea market. At the flea market Amir meets Soraya, a young Afghan woman who intrigues him. She is the topic of gossip in the community, apparently because of a previous romantic relationship that ended poorly.

Chapter 12:

Amir finally finds the courage to speak to Soraya after constantly thinking about her. They talk about literature and their ambitions, and Amir admires Soraya. Their interactions spark gossip among others at the flea market.

Meanwhile, Baba gets sick and is soon diagnosed with cancer. He refuses to go for chemotherapy and gradually becomes more emaciated, but insists on keeping his illness a secret. General Sahib and his family find out about it when Baba collapses one day and is sent to the hospital. When Baba is discharged, Amir asks him to request Soraya's hand in marriage from her father, General Taheri. Baba agrees and Soraya discloses to Amir her secret that she once ran away with an Afghan man who was doing drugs. Amir does not change his mind about marrying her but rather feels envious that she, unlike him, has the courage to reveal her secret.

Chapter 13:

The two families proceed with the traditional engagement customs the next evening, but the ceremony is shortened due to Baba's debilitating health. Baba is happy to see Amir get married and he spends nearly all his life savings on the wedding. After the wedding, Soraya suggests that she move in with Amir and Baba so that she can take care of Baba. The two get along very well. After a month, Baba passes away.

Amir and Soraya find an apartment of their own and they both enroll in university, despite the General's disapproval of Soraya wanting to become a teacher. Amir soon becomes a published novelist and Soraya's family celebrates his achievement. However, the couple also discover that they are unable to conceive children, which devastates them. Amir regards this as a form of punishment for his past mistakes. The infertility begins to take a toll on their marriage and Soraya and her family cannot fathom the idea of adoption.

Chapter 14:

Amir tells Soraya more about the call that he described to the readers in Chapter 1. The more he reflects on Khan's words "(Come, there is a way to be good again"), the more Amir is convinced that Khan knows about everything that he has done to Hassan. Soraya's father becomes ill and their relationship improves as she cares for him, but Soraya and Amir's marriage continues to be affected by their infertility.

The week before he leaves to visit Pakistan, Amir has a pleasant dream about Hassan, which he recounts to the reader.

Chapter 15: Amir finally gets to meet Rahim Khan in Pakistan. While Amir updates Khan about his life in America, Khan tells him about the dire state of Afghanistan under the Taliban. Although the Taliban were treated like heroes after they overthrew the Northern Alliance and brought peace, this peace was merely an illusion. The Taliban have since wreaked havoc on the lives of the Afghan people with acts of violence. Amir also learns that Rahim Khan is dying, and offers to take him to America to seek medical treatment. However, Khan declines and instead wants to tell Amir about Hassan.

Thought Questions (students consider while they read)

1. How is the issue of gender inequality brought out in this section?
2. How was Rahim Khan more of a father figure to Amir than Baba?
3. How does Soraya's presence in Amir's life cause him to grow and reflect more?
4. In what ways are the Taliban portrayed in this section?
5. How has Amir's relationship with Baba changed?

Vocabulary (in order of appearance)

Chapter 11, pg. 125:

- dissertations: long theses, often written to complete a PhD

Chapter 11, pg. 124:

- ire: extreme anger

Chapter 11, pg. 125:

- de facto: in fact

Chapter 11, pg. 126:

- cretin: a stupid person

Chapter 11, pg. 129:

- intertwined: inextricably connected
- tabla: an Indian musical instrument resembling a drum.

Chapter 11, pg. 129:

- harmonium: a musical instrument which takes the form of an organ

Chapter 11, pg. 131:

- mortarboard: a flat-topped cap with tassels used by graduates

Chapter 11, pg. 132:

- permeated: spread through

Chapter 11, pg. 134:

- antidote: cure

Chapter 11, pg. 137:

- ramshackle: worn and in disrepair

Chapter 12, pg. 144:

- portly: fat

Chapter 12, pg. 145:

- tenets: beliefs or principles

Chapter 12, pg.:

- teetering: bordering unsteadily

Chapter 12, pg. 150:

- fawning: giving attention to someone out of admiration

Chapter 12, pg. 155:

- bronchoscopy: a medical procedure which involves inserting a tube into the windpipe
- pathology: the study of disease

Chapter 12, pg. 156:

- palliative: alleviating pain or discomfort

Chapter 12, pg. 157:

- reticence: reservedness, shyness
- furtive: characterized by secrecy

Chapter 12, pg. 158:

- receded: went back

Chapter 12, pg. 165:

- chastise: to criticize harshly

Chapter 13, pg. 181:

- chagrin: extreme unhappiness

Chapter 13, pg. 185:

- trundling: moving heavily and noisily

Chapter 13, pg. 193:

- protracted: extended

Chapter 14, pg. 193:

- soliloquy: a speech given by one person directly to the audience

Chapter 15, pg. 195:

- garrulous: excessively talkative

Chapter 15, pg. 199:

- gnarled: rough and twisted

Chapter 15, pg. 200:

- collateral: at the side

Additional Homework

1. Ask students to do additional research on the impact of the Taliban in Afghanistan and write a reaction paper (1-2 pages) about what they learn.

Day 3 - Discussion of Thought Questions

1. How is the issue of gender inequality brought out in this section?

   Time: 10 mins

   Discussion: The issue is mostly depicted in the community's treatment of Soraya. She is viewed as a "tainted" woman in the eyes of the community for having run away with a man without being married. Even after she returns to her family, the stigmatization does not stop and the members of the community continues to gossip about her and judge her. She argues that the same treatment would not have befallen a man, had he been in her shoes because the Afghan community is more forgiving of men's licentious behavior, while they have rigid expectations that omen be pure and virtuous.

2. How was Rahim Khan more of a father figure to Amir than Baba?

   Time: 5 mins

   Discussion: Khan believed more in Amir's abilities than Baba did. Khan was willing to listen to Amir's stories. He even encouraged Amir to nurture his talent for writing by giving him a notebook to continue writing his stories in. Khan also stood up for Amir when Baba was making disparaging comments about him. During Amir's twelfth birthday, Khan sensed that Amir was having a difficult time and offered to be his confidante, a role he fulfilled in later years.

3. How does Soraya's presence in Amir's life cause him to grow and reflect more?

   Time: 10 mins

   Discussion: When Soraya reveals her secret to Amir, he cannot help but compare himself to her. He admires her courage and is envious of her because she is freed from her secret, while Amir's secret continues to burden him. Also, because of his own transgressions, he does not feel entitled to judge Soraya for her mistakes but rather accepts her wholeheartedly. Also, when he gets married to Soraya, he thinks about Hassan and whether he has married, which is evidence of his growing capacity to think of others and be less self-centered. These reactions of Amir is symbolic of a more mature character who has grown.

4. In what ways are the Taliban portrayed in this section?

   Time: 5 mins

   Discussion: The portrayal of the Taliban is very much derived from Rahim Khan's account of them. He describes them as violent and aggressive and despotic in the rule of the country. Under their rule, the people have much to fear. They have no regard for human rights or respect for the elderly, as evidenced from the way that one of the soldiers had wounded Khan for no justifiable reason.

5. How has Amir's relationship with Baba changed?

   Time: 5-7 min

   Discussion: Amir and Baba's relationship has progressed and improved in some ways since coming to America. Without the presence of Hassan and his friends, Baba devotes his attention more fully to Amir, celebrating his graduation from junior college and boasting about his writing to his friends. When Amir gets married, Baba says it is the happiest moment of his life.

Day 3 - Short Answer Quiz

1. What did Baba once tell Amir about Pashtuns?

2. What was Baba's political stance towards the Russians in Afghanistan?

3. Why does Baba refuse food stamps?

4. Why does Amir embrace America?

5. What does Amir do that impresses Khanum Taheri?

6. Why does Soraya want to be a teacher?

7. How does Amir first start making conversation with Soraya?

8. Why did Baba have a problem with Dr. Schneider?

9. How did Soraya react when her father finds her and the man she eloped with?

10. Why do Soraya and Amir shorten their engagement period?

Short Answer Quiz Key

1. He told Amir that they may be hardheaded and far too proud, but they would stand by one another in times of need.
2. He felt that they were doing a poor job of running the country, especially Leonid Brezhnev, whom Baba felt was an incompetent ruler.
3. He wants to keep his dignity and says that he would rather work to earn money for food than receive it for free.
4. America lets Amir feel free from the ghosts of his past, providing him with a chance to start anew.
5. He declines her offer to sit down and eat some peaches, which Khanum Taheri feels is the polite thing to do.
6. Soraya once taught a servant to read and write, and she found it very fulfilling.
7. He asks Soraya to relay a message to her father.
8. Dr. Schneider was Russian-American, and Baba detested Russians from his experiences with them in Afghanistan.
9. She went hysterical, screaming and yelling and saying that she hated her father.
10. They shorten their engagement so that Baba can attend, since his health is deteriorating.

Day 3 - Crossword Puzzle

ACROSS

4. asking for a woman's hand in marriage
6. what Amir felt when Rahim Khan mentioned Hassan
11. the hired help who Soraya had taught to read and write
12. the state where Baba and Amir had moved to
16. the place where Rahim Khan was struck on the forehead by a Talib
17. excessively talkative
18. to criticize harshly
19. characterized by secrecy
20. the problem which plagued Amir and Soraya

DOWN

1. the place which Soraya had eloped to with the Afghan man
2. quietness about thoughts and feelings
3. fat
5. alleviating pain but not curing it
7. giving attention to someone out of admiration
8. the fruit which Khanum Taheri offers Amir and which he declines
9. in fact
10. beliefs or principles
13. the occupation to which Soraya aspires
14. the name of Baba's illness
15. a person suffering from a mental deficiency or stupidity

Crossword Puzzle Answer Key

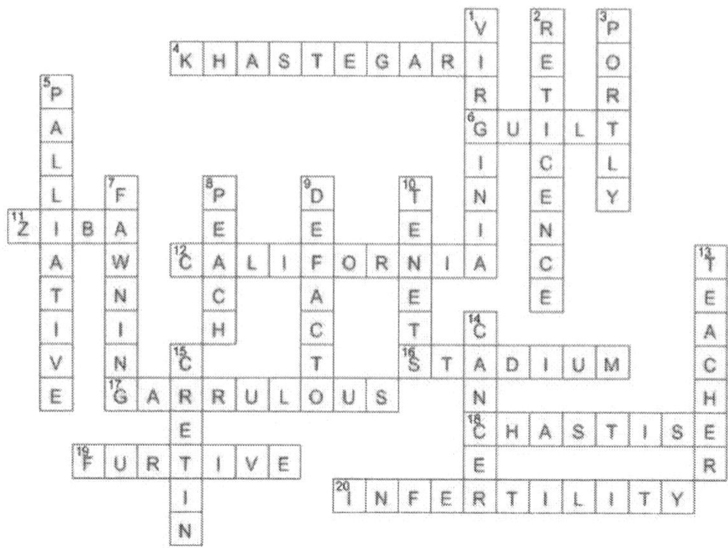

ACROSS

4. asking for a woman's hand in marriage
6. what Amir felt when Rahim Khan mentioned Hassan
11. the hired help who Soraya had taught to read and write
12. the state where Baba and Amir had moved to
16. the place where Rahim Khan was struck on the forehead by a Talib
17. excessively talkative
18. to criticize harshly
19. characterized by secrecy
20. the problem which plagued Amir and Soraya

DOWN

1. the place which Soraya had eloped to with the Afghan man
2. quietness about thoughts and feelings
3. fat
5. alleviating pain but not curing it
7. giving attention to someone out of admiration
8. the fruit which Khanum Taheri offers Amir and which he declines
9. in fact
10. beliefs or principles
13. the occupation to which Soraya aspires
14. the name of Baba's illness
15. a person suffering from a mental deficiency or stupidity

Day 3 - Vocabulary Quiz

Terms

1. ____ dissertations
2. ____ ire
3. ____ de facto
4. ____ cretin
5. ____ intertwined
6. ____ tabla
7. ____ harmonium
8. ____ mortarboard
9. ____ permeated
10. ____ bronchoscopy
11. ____ palliative
12. ____ furtive
13. ____ receded
14. ____ chastise
15. ____ chagrin
16. ____ trundling
17. ____ protracted
18. ____ soliloquy
19. ____ garrulous
20. ____ gnarled

Answers

A. went back
B. extended
C. characterized by secrecy
D. extreme anger
E. long theses, often written to complete a PhD
F. an Indian musical instrument resembling a drum.
G. a legal phrase referring to something that occurs in actuality but is not enshrined in law
H. to criticize harshly
I. excessively talkative
J. extreme unhappiness
K. a speech given by one person directly to the audience
L. a musical instrument similar to an organ
M. a flat-topped cap with tassels worn by graduates
N. inextricably connected
O. spread through
P. alleviating pain or discomfort
Q. rough and twisted
R. a stupid person
S. moving heavily and noisily
T. a medical procedure which involves inserting a tube into the windpipe

Vocabulary Quiz Answer Key

1. E
2. D
3. G
4. R
5. N
6. F
7. L
8. M
9. O
10. T
11. P
12. C
13. A
14. H
15. J
16. S
17. B
18. K
19. I
20. Q

Day 3 - Classroom Activities

1. The Taliban in Afghanistan

    Kind of Activity: Research
    Objective: Students will understand Afghanistan's recent history, particularly the rise of the Taliban.
    Common Core State Standards: CCSS.ELA-Literacy.RL.9-10.1, CCSS.ELA-Literacy.RL.9-10.2, CCSS.ELA-Literacy.RL.9-10.6
    Time: 30-40 mins

    Structure:

    Show the class a clip from news report or documentary about recent Afghan history, particularly the country's history under the Taliban. After watching the clip, facilitate a discussion about how this media portrait of Afghanistan and the Taliban compares with the portrayal found in *The Kite Runner*.

    Next, have students do their own research on the subject using books, newspapers, magazines, Internet sources, and video clips provided by the instructor. The students should take notes as they peruse these sources, jotting down their thoughts about how the depictions provided match up with what they have read in the novel.

    Come together as a class to discuss what the students have learned from the exercise and how their perceptions of Afghanistan might have changed based on the novel and their research.

    Ideans for Differentiated Instruction:

    -Provide sources of varying length and complexity so that students can choose appropriate sources for their skill level.

    -Provide a mix of print, audio, video, and interactive resources to engage different kinds of learners.

    -Provide scaffolding questions and graphic organizers for student note-taking purposes.

    Assessment Ideas:

    -Have students turn in their notes and answers to questions for instructor evaluation.

    -Assess student participation in the class discussion, and walk through the classroom during the activity so that you can be aware of any issues that might come up, or any students who might need guidance.

2. Amir's Growth

Kind of Activity: Creative Writing
Objective: Students should be able to trace the significant developments in Amir's character based on close reading of the text.
Common Core State Standards: CCSS.ELA-Literacy.RL.9-10.3
Time: 30 mins

Structure:

Have students write a letter from the adult Amir to himself when he was a child. The letter should reflect generally on Amir's growth as a person, and on what he has learned and wants to impart to his former self. Students should include reflections on at least two major incidents from the novel, whether they are narrated in the text itself or merely mentioned by the narrator in passing. The letter should capture, as much as possible, Amir's narrative voice and point of view, but more importantly, how he has changed over the course of the novel.

After giving them time to write, ask the students to share parts of their letters aloud and discuss the process of writing them, including why they chose certain parts of the narrative to focus on, how they got into Amir's voice, etc.

Ideans for Differentiated Instruction:

-If some students struggle with writing, creating a brief audio or video letter might be an alternative.

-For students who are having difficulty, provide prompts and relevant questions to guide their thinking, or point them toward relevant textual passages.

Assessment Ideas:
-Peer Evaluation: Students exchange their letters with a partner, who will evaluate their work based on specific criteria given by the instructor.

Day 4 - Reading Assignment

Read Chapters 16-20.

Common Core Objectives

- 1) CCSS.ELA-Literacy.RL.9-10.1 Cite strong and thorough textual evidence to support analysis of what the text says explicitly as well as inferences drawn from the text.

  2) CCSS.ELA-Literacy.RL.9-10.2 Determine a theme or central idea of a text and analyze in detail its development over the course of the text, including how it emerges and is shaped and refined by specific details; provide an objective summary of the text.

  3) CCSS.ELA-Literacy.RL.9-10.7 Analyze the representation of a subject or a key scene in two different artistic mediums, including what is emphasized or absent in each treatment

Note that it is perfectly fine to expand any day's work into two days depending on the characteristics of the class, particularly if the class will engage in all of the suggested classroom exercises and activities and discuss all of the thought questions.

Content Summary for Teachers

Chapter 16: This chapter is narrated from the perspective of Rahim Khan. He tells the story of how he sought out Hassan in Hazarajat because he was lonely and did not want to live alone. Khan finds out that Hassan married a woman named Farzana and that Ali died in a land mine incident. Hassan asks Rahim Khan about Amir frequently. After several years, Hassan and Farzana have a child and name him Sohrab, after the heroic figure in Shanamah. Hassan's mother, Sanaubar, shows up in order to reunite with him, and ultimately both Farzana and Hassan welcome Sanaubar into their household. Khan also mentions that Hassan has taught his son how to use a slingshot and takes him kite-running on the weekends. The chapter ends on a grim note, when Khan recalls how the Taliban banned kite fighting when they gained control over the country and how they massacred the Hazaras.

Chapter 17:

Khan's narrative in the previous chapter had piqued Amir's curiosity, and he begins to inquire about Hassan. In response, Khan shows Amir a Polaroid picture of Hassan and Sohrab and a letter that Hassan has written to Amir. Hassan's letter is affectionate and it is clear that he still regards himself as Amir's loyal servant.

It is only after Amir reads the letter twice that Khan informs him that Hassan and Farzana were killed by Taliban officials and their son placed in an orphanage in Kabul. Khan then urges Amir to bring Sohrab back to Peshawar, with the help of an American couple. Amir is reluctant, but Khan then reveals that Amir and Hassan are half-brothers. Amir is unable to accept this truth and leaves the apartment in a troubled state of mind.

Chapter 18: As Amir considers the truth that he has just discovered, he reasons that this must be why Baba treated Hassan so well all this time. He feels betrayed by Baba, but it also dawns on him that he and Baba are alike: had he not betrayed Hassan, Baba might have brought both Ali and Hassan to America and escaped death at the hands of the Taliban. Amir thus sees an opportunity for redemption in taking Sohrab from the orphanage. He informs Khan about his decision.

Chapter 19: Rahim Khan asks a man named Farid to drive Amir to Kabul. Amir gets no sympathy or respect at all from Farid, who sees Amir as a privileged outsider. Once he knows about Amir's plans to retrieve Sohrab, however, Farid comes around and even volunteers to help Amir. That night when Amir stays in Wahid's house, he has a dream about Hassan's murder and wakes up horrified. The next day as he steps out of the house, he feels strangely connected to the land. Amir overhears Wahid talking to his wife and realizes that their children did not have enough food to eat because they fed him. To compensate, Amir deliberately leaves a stack of money under his pillow when he departs.

Chapter 20: When Amir finally arrives in Kabul with Farid, he is appalled by the poverty he sees and the Taliban who walk around on patrol. They find the orphanage and discover that Zaman, its proprietor, has sold Sohrab to a Taliban official. Farid is enraged and starts attacking Zaman. Amir intervenes, pointing out to Farid that the children are watching. Zaman then explains that he needs the money to provide for the children in the orphanage. He describes the Talib official as a man wearing sunglasses, and tells them to go to Ghazi stadium the following day where they will find him.

Thought Questions (students consider while they read)

1. What emotions are behind Amir's reactions when he finds out that Hassan is his half-brother?
2. What changes have taken place in Afghanistan since Amir left?
3. How does Sanaubar try to redeem herself? Why do you think she has not returned until so late in her life?
4. Examine the use of one or two symbols in this section (e.g. dreams, the pomegranate tree, poverty, etc.)
5. What is the significance of the narrative shifting to Rahim Khan's perspective in Chapter 16?

Vocabulary (in order of appearance)

Chapter 16, pg. 205:

- affable: friendly

Chapter 16, pg. 211:

- skillet: a small frying pan

Chapter 16, pg. 219:

- herringbone: a weave pattern that makes a 'V' shape

Chapter 16, pg. 224:

- swathed: wrapped up, usually in cloth

Chapter 17, pg. 214:

- parched: extremely dry

Chapter 17, pg. 215:

- beneficent: generous

Chapter 17, pg. 221:

- limbo: in a position that is in between two entities

Chapter 18, pg. 224:

- samovar: a decorative tea urn

Chapter 18, pg. 226:

- oblivion: a state of being unaware or unconscious

Chapter 19, pg. 230:

- rueful: sorrowful

Chapter 19, pg. 231:

- ruminate: to ponder deeply
- haunches: buttocks and thighs

- emaciated: unhealthily thin and weak

Chapter 19, pg. 233:

- arduous: tedious

Chapter 19, pg. 234:

- poplar: a type of tree

Chapter 19, pg. 236:

- contemptuous: hateful

Chapter 20, pg. 243:

- relic: an old object that brings back memories of the past

Chapter 20, pg. 245:

- thoroughfare: a road which leads to another road

Chapter 20, pg. 247:

- unadulterated: not tainted

Chapter 20, pg. 252:

- cursory: slight and short

Additional Homework

1. Students could write a critical review of the entire movie, based on how faithful it is to the novel.

Day 4 - Discussion of Thought Questions

1. What emotions are behind Amir's reactions when he finds out that Hassan is his half-brother?

   Time: 5 mins

   Discussion: Amir is completely shocked and feels betrayed by Baba and Rahim Khan for keeping the truth from him for so long. He lashes out at Khan, calling him and Baba liars. Baba had once told him that there was only one sin, which was theft, and had admonished thieves, but Amir now says that Baba was in fact a thief himself. It also dawns upon Amir that he and Baba are not that different after all. Eventually, Amir is able to accept the truth and is understand why Baba had always showered Hassan with attention and affection even though he was just a servant.

2. What changes have taken place in Afghanistan since Amir left?

   Time: 5 mins

   Discussion: Amir notices that there are no longer any kites or kite shops, the trees have been cut down in Jadeh Maywand, the orphanage that Baba built has also been destroyed. There are also more beggars and more poverty in general, and the Taliban officers are a new and unwelcome addition to his home country.

3. How does Sanaubar try to redeem herself? Why do you think she has not returned until so late in her life?

   Time: 5 mins

   Discussion: She delivers Hassan's child and helps to raise him, constantly doting on him. She also makes it a point to ask for Hassan's forgiveness for abandoning him. She takes the opportunity to get to know him better and to bond with him in the remaining years of her life. As for why she has returned at this late date, students might speculate on how her guilt has affected her ability to come to terms with her actions and how her story mirrors Amir's.

4. Examine the use of one or two symbols in this section (e.g. dreams, the pomegranate tree, poverty, etc.)

   Time: 10 mins

   Discussion: Amir's dream about Hassan being murdered could be a manifestation of his guilt and his feeling that he was somehow responsible for Hassan's death. Also, the pomegranate tree that Hassan and Sohrab sit under could represent love and familial connection, since it was the same tree that Hassan and Amir sat under as children. The trees that have been cut down in Jadeh Mayward, as well as the barrenness of the pomegranate tree, could represent the desolate state of Afghanistan since the Taliban have gained control of the country. The lack of food in Wahid's household could represent the broader poverty and strife that many Afghans had to endure.

5. What is the significance of the narrative shifting to Rahim Khan's perspective in Chapter 16?

   Time: 5 mins

   Discussion: This switch in point of view allows the reader to gain a different perspective for the first time, perhaps a clearer perspective given the emotional nature of these events for Amir. The reader can also sympathize more easily with Khan's struggles of loneliness and his debilitating health conditions. Having Khan narrate this chapter also underscores his pivotal role in the novel: without him, Amir would never have found out the truth about Baba, Hassan and Sohrab.

Day 4 - Short Answer Quiz

1. Why did Hassan want to ensure that Sohrab knew how to read?

2. Why was Sohrab not in the orphanage that Zaman was in charge of?

3. Why were Wahid's children staring at Amir's food?

4. Why did Farid start to treat Amir better?

5. What did the beggar on the street first say to Amir?

6. Why did Hassan not want to move into the house with Rahim Khan?

7. Why did Hassan name his son Sohrab?

____

8. How did Amir describe Sohrab to Zaman?

____

9. According to Hassan, why was Farzana abused at the bazaar?

____

10. According to Rahim Khan, why didn't the neighbours say anything about Hassan and Farzana's death?

____

Short Answer Quiz Key

1. He wanted Sohrab to be smarter than he was and to hopefully have a better life than he ever did.
2. A Talib official had taken Sohrab away in exchange for a sum of money that he had paid to Zaman.
3. There was not enough food for them to eat and they were probably eyeing Amir's food as they were hungry.
4. He found out that the real reason that Amir returned to Afghanistan was to find his half-nephew in an orphanage and to bring him to Peshawar where there will be people to take care of him. Farid probably thought that this was an honourable deed.
5. He told Amir that Farid was giving him good advice to not stare at the Taliban.
6. He respected Amir and he did not want Amir to think that he was taking over his place in the house should Amir return.
7. Sohrab was the name of Hassan's favourite hero from the book, Shahnamah.
8. He described him as a boy who was very good with the slingshot, called his grandmother Sasa and that he knew how to read and write.
9. She had asked a vendor how much the potatoes cost in what was considered a loud voice by the Taliban official. He had struck her, saying that the Ministry of Vice and Virtue prohibited women from speaking in a loud voice.
10. They feared the Taliban and it was not worth risking their lives for a pair of Hazara servants.

Day 4 - Crossword Puzzle

ACROSS

4. distinctive item worn by Taliban official who had taken Sohrab away
6. Rahim Khan gives this to Amir along with a Polaroid
10. a small frying pan
11. tedious
12. Amir encounters one such person who claims to have known his mother
16. a furnished tea urn
17. sorrowful
18. Hassan's wife
19. the name of Hassan's mother
20. Amir leaves this under his pillow before he leaves Wahid's house

DOWN

1. hateful
2. Amir dreams about him while he is sleeping in Wahid's house
3. to ponder deeply
5. Farid chides Amir for doing this they encounter Taliban officials on the street
7. an old object that brings back memories of the past
8. untainted
9. the man who drives Amir around in Afghanistan
13. slight and short
14. the man who runs the orphanage
15. friendly

Crossword Puzzle Answer Key

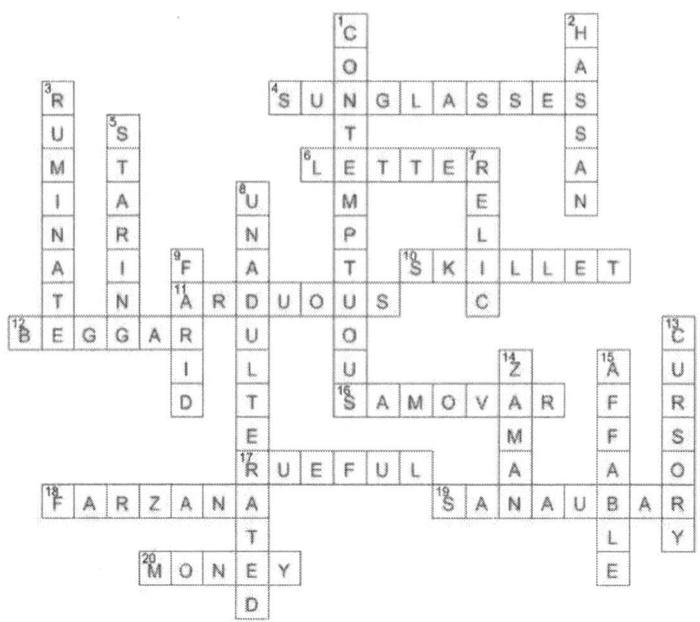

ACROSS

4. distinctive item worn by Taliban official who had taken Sohrab away
6. Rahim Khan gives this to Amir along with a Polaroid
10. a small frying pan
11. tedious
12. Amir encounters one such person who claims to have known his mother
16. a furnished tea urn
17. sorrowful
18. Hassan's wife
19. the name of Hassan's mother
20. Amir leaves this under his pillow before he leaves Wahid's house

DOWN

1. hateful
2. Amir dreams about him while he is sleeping in Wahid's house
3. to ponder deeply
5. Farid chides Amir for doing this they encounter Taliban officials on the street
7. an old object that brings back memories of the past
8. untainted
9. the man who drives Amir around in Afghanistan
13. slight and short
14. the man who runs the orphanage
15. friendly

Day 4 - Vocabulary Quiz

Terms	Answers
1. ____ affable	A. a weave pattern that makes a 'V' shape
2. ____ skillet	B. friendly
3. ____ herringbone	C. generous
4. ____ swathed	D. wrapped up, usually in cloth
5. ____ parched	E. a furnished tea urn
6. ____ beneficent	F. to ponder deeply
7. ____ limbo	G. a state of being unaware or unconscious
8. ____ oblivion	H. extremely dry
9. ____ ruminate	I. slight and short
10. ____ emaciated	J. unhealthily thin and weak
11. ____ arduous	K. a road which leads to another road
12. ____ poplar	L. hateful
13. ____ contemptuous	M. in a position that is in between two entities
14. ____ relic	N. tedious
15. ____ samovar	O. untainted
16. ____ thoroughfare	P. a type of tree
17. ____ unadulterated	Q. a small frying pan
18. ____ cursory	R. an old object that brings back memories of the past

Vocabulary Quiz Answer Key

1. B
2. Q
3. A
4. D
5. H
6. C
7. M
8. G
9. F
10. J
11. N
12. P
13. L
14. R
15. E
16. K
17. O
18. I

Day 4 - Classroom Activities

1. The Truth Will Set You Free

Kind of Activity: Collaborative Writing
Objective: Students should be able to present a nuanced argument based on evidence from the text.
Common Core State Standards: CCSS.ELA-Literacy.RL.9-10.1, CCSS.ELA-Literacy.RL.9-10.2
Time: 30-45 mins

Structure:

It is often said that "the truth will set you free." In this activity, students will evaluate this statement with regard to the characters' experiences in the novel. First, ask students whether they have heard this statement before and what they think it means. Then ask them how it might apply to the characters and situations in *The Kite Runner*.

The power of truth and the pain of secrecy are common threads throughout the novel, so students can choose to evaluate the statement with regard to any number of characters and their experiences. For instance:

-The fact that Hassan is Amir's half-brother (this could be discussed in relation to Amir, Baba, or Rahim Khan)

-Amir's cowardice during Hassan's assault

-Soraya's affair and elopement

Students should work in pairs and develop arguments about the proposed statement as it relates to the novel. One student in each pair will take the pro side, while the other takes the con. The instructor should assign students to a particular side at random.

After the students discuss and develop their arguments in pairs, bring the class together to talk about the issues in a class-wide setting.

Ideans for Differentiated Instruction:

-Provide scaffolding questions or point students toward relevant textual evidence for their arguments.

-Allow students to prepare by writing down notes, using a laptop to type up their ideas, or using dictation software if it is available.

Assessment Ideas:

-Have students turn in their notes (in whatever format they have utilized) for evaluation by the instructor.

-Assess the students' performance during the in-class discussion and their ability to work with their partner as you observe each pair during the course of the activity.

2. Film Adaptations

Kind of Activity: Classwide Discussion
Objective: Students should be able to compare and contrast different presentations of the material in the text and use their creativity to imagine alternative presentations
Common Core State Standards: CCSS.ELA-Literacy.RL.9-10.7
Time: 30-40 mins

Structure:

Show a short clip from the film adaptation of *The Kite Runner*. Ask students to comment on the clip and how it portrays the events of the novel. Questions to guide the discussion include:

1) What do you like about the director's portrayal? Why?

2) What do you not like about the portrayal? Why?

3) If you could change anything about this portrayal, what would it be?

4) What aspects of the novel might have been difficult to adapt for film? What aspects of it might lend themselves well to film?

Students should defend their opinions with evidence from the text, and discuss other film adaptations that they feel have been successful.

Ideans for Differentiated Instruction:

-Make sure to engage more reserved students in the class discussion by asking them questions directly.

-Provide scaffolding questions to students who need more guidance.

Assessment Ideas:

-Have students rewrite a scene from the movie, based on their own understanding of the novel.

-Have students watch the rest of the film on their own and write a review.

Day 5 - Reading Assignment

Read Chapters 21-25.

Common Core Objectives

- 1)CCSS.ELA-Literacy.RL.9-10.5 Analyze how an author's choices concerning how to structure a text, order events within it (e.g., parallel plots), and manipulate time (e.g., pacing, flashbacks) create such effects as mystery, tension, or surprise.

  2)CCSS.ELA-Literacy.RL.9-10.6 Analyze a particular point of view or cultural experience reflected in a work of literature from outside the United States, drawing on a wide reading of world literature.

Note that it is perfectly fine to expand any day's work into two days depending on the characteristics of the class, particularly if the class will engage in all of the suggested classroom exercises and activities and discuss all of the thought questions.

Content Summary for Teachers

Chapter 21:

As Amir and Farid drive towards Pashtunistan, Amir spots a dead body hanging on a street, and they also come upon a man who is trying to sell off his limb. Farid explains that one would be able to get good money from such a sale to feed one's children.

As soon as Amir spots his old house, he is transported back in time to a memory of his childhood during one of his adventures with Hassan. Although he feels alienated from the house and Farid urges him to forget about the past, he is still determined to find the pomegranate tree he and Hassan used to sit under.

That night, Farid and Amir stay in a run-down hotel and bond over stories about their lives and jokes about politics. Amir is unable to sleep, thinking about what a hopeless place Afghanistan has become. The next morning, both of them go to Ghazi Stadium to look for the Taliban official with the sunglasses. They are faced with a public punishment scene where a couple is being stoned to death for committing adultery. After the stoning, the bodies are cleared and the second half of a soccer game resumes. Farid manages to make an appointment to meet with the Taliban official later that afternoon.

Chapter 22:

Amir meets with the Talib who has taken Sohrab, and the experience is dangerous and disturbing for him. The Taliban guards tear away Amir's beard and the Talib official questions Amir's loyalty to Afghanistan, threatening to arrest him for treason. Amir keeps reiterating that he has come for Sohrab. Finally, the Talib has his guards bring Sohrab out, and they make Sohrab perform a dance for them with bells around his ankles. The official then orders the guards to leave the room and after they do, the official touches Sohrab suggestively.

The Talib asks Amir a question about Baba, and Amir realizes that it is Assef. Assef tells him the story of how he joined the Taliban after surviving his tough jail sentence, seeing it as God's will for him to join the mission. Assef offers to give up Sohrab if Amir submits to a beating with brass knuckles. As Assef beats him, Amir begins to laugh as he finally feels a sense of liberation, as if he has atoned for his sins. Sohrab intervenes by hitting Assef in the eye with a slingshot. They drive away with Farid.

Chapter 23:

Amir is still reeling from the pain of his beating, and he is not always fully aware of his surroundings. He soon realizes that he has had surgery and is in the hospital recuperating. When Sohrab and Farid come to visit him, Amir properly introduces himself to Sohrab, but the child already knows about him from Hassan's stories.

Farid informs Amir that Rahim Khan is no longer at his house, but has left a letter. In his letter, Khan apologizes and explains that Baba withheld his affections from Amir because he saw himself in him, and he felt guilty that he could not openly love Hassan as his son. Khan also says that God will forgive them all and that Amir should also learn to forgive himself. He has left some money for Amir in a safe in Peshawar, and he implores Amir to let him spend his dying days alone.

Chapter 24:

Amir and Sohrab check into a hotel in Islamabad. Before Farid leaves, Amir hands him an envelope with a wad of cash to thank him for all his help. Farid is shocked by the amount of money. The next morning, Sohrab is nowhere to be found and Amir panics. He eventually finds Sohrab near a mosque in the city. While they walk back to the hotel, Sohrab and Amir have a heartfelt conversation and Sohrab reveals to him how much he misses his parents, his grandmother and Rahim Khan, but he is glad that they are not around to see how tainted he has become. Amir keeps reassuring him that he is not at all dirty and that he will not go to hell for hurting Assef.

While comforting a sobbing Sohrab, Amir asks him if he would like to come live in America. Amir also decides to tell Soraya what he has learned about Hassan, and Soraya agrees to take him in. However, Amir finds that he needs the death certificates of Sohrab's parents in order to adopt him. Just as Amir receives some good news from Soraya, he finds Sohrab bleeding in the bathtub--he had tried to commit suicide, distraught at the idea of having to return to an orphanage.

Chapter 25:

Sohrab is sent to the emergency room in critical condition. Amir, who feels helpless, begins to pray for the first time in a long time. He promises God that he will lead a more religious life should Sohrab survive. When Amir finally gets to speak to Sohrab, all he says is that he is tired of everything and wants his old life back. He has clearly lost the will to carry on living. Amir does his best to continue reassuring him about the future and asks for his forgiveness, but Sohrab does not respond.

A week later, they arrive in America. Soraya welcomes Sohrab with open arms and does her best to be a maternal figure to him, despite his failure to reciprocate. General Tahiri, on the other hand, is less welcoming. To cope with Sohrab's silence, Amir and Soraya involve themselves in Afghan community projects after the United States launches attacks on Afghanistan following the September 11 bombings of the World Trade Center. Shortly after the Afghan new year, Amir buys Sohrab a kite and shows him how to fly it, all the while telling him about Hassan and how he used to be the best kite-runner. Although Sohrab does not say anything, Amir notices that he does smile slightly. The novel ends with Amir running a kite for Sohrab, after telling him, "For you a thousand times over."

Thought Questions (students consider while they read)

1. Why is it important that Hosseini includes graphic, macabre imagery in narrating the scenes of driving around in Afghanistan?
2. What is the role of the flash-forward employed in Chapter 22 while Assef is beating Amir?
3. Forgiveness is a major theme in this section of the novel. What message(s) do you see about forgiveness here?
4. How does Sohrab's attitude toward Amir change over time?
5. What does Amir mean when he says that "life is not a Hindi movie"?

Vocabulary (in order of appearance)

Chapter 21, pg. 261:

- pylons: towers or tall pillars used as directional guides

Chapter 21, pg. 263:

- scampered: ran quickly and lightly

Chapter 21, pg. 264:

- mosaic: a pattern made up of many colors, often made of tile
- crevasses: cracks

Chapter 21, pg. 265:

- succulent: juicy

Chapter 21, pg. 268:

- flogging: beating someone brutally, usually with a whip

Chapter 21, pg. 270:

- sanctity: sacred quality

Chapter 22, pg. 275:

- prudence: quality of being careful

Chapter 22, pg. 276:

- retracted: withdrew
- en masse: all together in large numbers

Chapter 22, pg. 277:

- tremulous: trembling

Chapter 22, pg. 278:

- unison: with one voice
- treason: betrayal

Chapter 22, pg. 281:

- surreal: having some realistic elements mixed with fantasy

Chapter 22, pg. 282:

- epiphany: a sudden realization of something

Chapter 22, pg. 283:

- bourgeoisie: the middle class in a society

Chapter 22, pg. 284:

- shrapnel: a fragment of a shell from an explosion

Chapter 22, pg. 296:

- hemorrhage: a great loss of blood

Chapter 23, pg. 297:

- laceration: a deep cut

Chapter 23, pg. 309:

- hodgepodge: a mixture

Chapter 24, pg. 313:

- carafe: a container with a wide, open mouth used to serve beverages

Chapter 24, pg. 316:

- reproachful: expressing blame

Chapter 24, pg. 320:

- convulsed: shook forcefully and uncontrollably

Chapter 24, pg. 329:

- squalid: extremely filthy
- prognosis: a medical prediction of a cause and recovery of an illness

Chapter 24, pg. 338:

- milieu: social environment

Chapter 24, pg. 339:

- asylum: refuge from harm or danger

Chapter 25, pg. 344:

- gurney: a stretcher with wheels

Chapter 25, pg. 353:

- replete: filled with

Chapter 25, pg. 358:

- locomotive: a vehicle used for moving trains

Chapter 25, pg. 365:

- eccentric: not the norm, slightly weird

Additional Homework

1. Have students draw relationship maps for the characters of the novel, focusing on characters whose relationships they feel elucidate a particular theme (e.g. forgiveness, redemption, friendship, etc.).

Day 5 - Discussion of Thought Questions

1. Why is it important that Hosseini includes graphic, macabre imagery in narrating the scenes of driving around in Afghanistan?

   Time: 5 mins

   Discussion: The macabre imagery foreshadows even greater amounts of violence that is about to take place later in Amir's travels in Afghanistan. It also makes the reader cognizant of the commonplace brutality and suffering endured in Afghanistan under the Taliban. The fact that Farid and others seem desensitized to the violence that Amir describes enhances the reader's emotional response to both the violence itself and the story being told.

2. What is the role of the flash-forward employed in Chapter 22 while Assef is beating Amir?

   Time: 5 mins

   Discussion: It lets the reader know that Amir survives the beating, but also builds suspense by interrupting the narrative at such a critical moment. Knowing that Amir survives, the reader is still anxious to find out how that unfolds.

3. Forgiveness is a major theme in this section of the novel. What message(s) do you see about forgiveness here?

   Time: 10 mins

   Discussion:

   Forgiveness is important in order to sustain relationships and to have peace of mind. Rahim Khan pleads with Amir to forgive him because he wants to have a peaceful death. Amir pleads with Sohrab to forgive him because he wants to start afresh and be a father figure.

Forgiveness of oneself is also important if one wishes to lead a fulfilling life. Khan advises Amir to forgive himself and to let go of his guilt, and to atone for that guilt instead by saving Sohrab. Amir heeds his advice and is able to provide Sohrab a better life.

4. How does Sohrab's attitude toward Amir change over time?

   Time: 10 mins

   Discussion: Sohrab is at first rather withdrawn and detached from Amir. However, he gradually warms up to Amir and they bond over games of panjpar. Sohrab is also able to confide in Amir, who constantly reassures him, making him feel safe and secure. Amir also talks at length about Hassan and how close he and Hassan used to be when they were children, which seems to comfort Sohrab. However, their interactions become troubled when Amir lets Sohrab know that he might need to go to an orphanage temporarily. Sohrab attempts suicide and stops communicating with those around him, including Amir. At the end of the novel, however, there a semblance of hope as Amir is able to make Sohrab smile again when the two go kite flying.

5. What does Amir mean when he says that "life is not a Hindi movie"?

   Time: 5 mins

   Discussion: Amir is reminding the readers that in real life, stories do not always end happily. Even if there are happy moments, there are always struggles as well. Life is also not neatly arranged, as in a movie. There is no definite beginning or ending and one just moves on with the passing of time. It is for this reason that the novel ends in the middle of many stories--that of Amir's life, his relationship with Sohrab, and his marriage to Soraya.

Day 5 - Short Answer Quiz

1. Why does Assef join the Taliban?

2. What crime did the couple commit that resulted in public stoning?

3. According to Rahim Khan, what good has come from Baba's remorse?

4. Why was it so difficult for Amir to adopt Sohrab while in Afghanistan?

5. Why didn't Sohrab want to be put into another orphanage?

6. What does Amir promise God if Sohrab lives?

7. How does Soraya treat Sohrab when he comes to America?

8. What is the "small miracle" Amir refers to at the end of the novel?

9. What does Kaka Sharif suggest Amir do to ease the adoption process?

10. How does the novel end?

Short Answer Quiz Key

1. After he survives abuse in prison, Assef believes that God wanted him to live in order to join the Taliban.
2. Adultery.
3. Khan believes that Baba's generosity toward the community was largely his attempt to redeem himself.
4. He had to legally prove that both of Sohrab's parents were dead, and it was virtually impossible to obtain death certificates in Afghanistan.
5. He was afraid that he would get mistreated again, and he was still traumatized and mistrustful, as he had been sexually assaulted by Assef and his men before.
6. He promises to be a more pious man, praying and fasting more regularly and even making a pilgrimage to the Holy Land.
7. She welcomes him and treats him as a son, trying to take care of his needs.
8. Amir manages to get Sohrab to fly a kit with him, and Sohrab smiles for the first time in a long time.
9. He suggests that Amir first bring Sohrab to America, because once he is there, there will be ways to keep him in the country.
10. It ends with Amir running and feeling liberated.

Day 5 - Crossword Puzzle

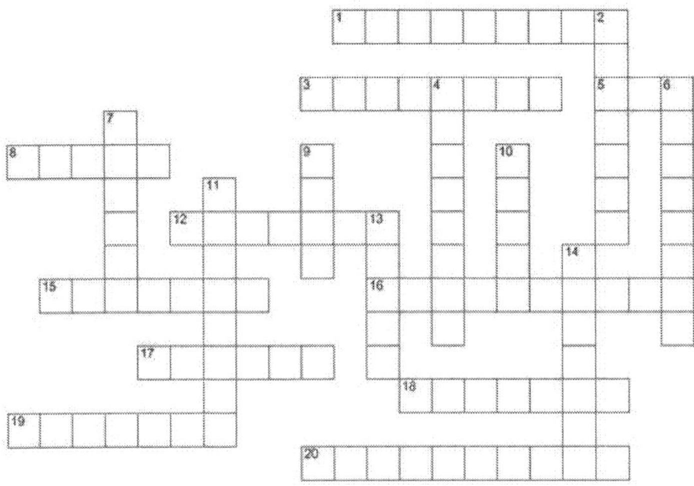

ACROSS

1. juicy
3. a fragment of a shell from an explosion
5. the part of the face where Sohrab had hit Assef
8. the one thing that had not changed in Kabul according to Amir
12. where Sohrab tries to commit suicide
15. the country which Amir wants to take Sohrab to
16. a deep cut
17. with one voice
18. extremely filthy and deplorable condition
19. where Amir enquires about adoption procedures
20. a mixture

DOWN

2. betrayal
4. quality of being careful
6. a sudden realization of something
7. where Amir finds Sohrab after he goes missing
9. Amir buys Sohrab this at the Lake Elizabeth Park
10. the place where the massacre of the Hazaras had occurred in August 1998
11. sacred quality
13. the objects that Sohrab was made to wear on his ankles
14. how the Taliban killed the adulterous couple in Ghazi Stadium

Crossword Puzzle Answer Key

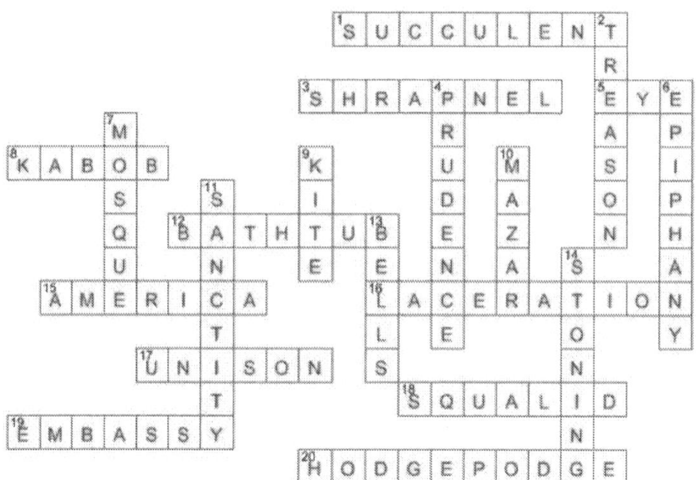

ACROSS

1. juicy
3. a fragment of a shell from an explosion
5. the part of the face where Sohrab had hit Assef
8. the one thing that had not changed in Kabul according to Amir
12. where Sohrab tries to commit suicide
15. the country which Amir wants to take Sohrab to
16. a deep cut
17. with one voice
18. extremely filthy and deplorable condition
19. where Amir enquires about adoption procedures
20. a mixture

DOWN

2. betrayal
4. quality of being careful
6. a sudden realization of something
7. where Amir finds Sohrab after he goes missing
9. Amir buys Sohrab this at the Lake Elizabeth Park
10. the place where the massacre of the Hazaras had occurred in August 1998
11. sacred quality
13. the objects that Sohrab was made to wear on his ankles
14. how the Taliban killed the adulterous couple in Ghazi Stadium

Day 5 - Vocabulary Quiz

Terms

1. ____ pylons
2. ____ scampered
3. ____ mosaic
4. ____ crevasses
5. ____ succulent
6. ____ flogging
7. ____ sanctity
8. ____ prudence
9. ____ retracted
10. ____ en masse
11. ____ tremulous
12. ____ unison
13. ____ treason
14. ____ surreal
15. ____ epiphany
16. ____ bourgeoisie
17. ____ shrapnel
18. ____ hemorrhage
19. ____ carafe
20. ____ milieu

Answers

A. all together in large numbers
B. cracks
C. towers or tall pillars used as directional guides
D. betrayal
E. a sudden realization of something
F. a container with a wide, open mouth used to serve beverages
G. beating someone brutally usually with a whip
H. withdrew
I. with one voice
J. the middle class in a society
K. some realistic elements mixed with fantasy
L. ran quickly and lightly
M. juicy
N. a pattern made up of many colors
O. trembling
P. a fragment of a shell from an explosion
Q. sacred quality
R. a great loss of blood
S. quality of being careful
T. social environment

Vocabulary Quiz Answer Key

1. C
2. L
3. N
4. B
5. M
6. G
7. Q
8. S
9. H
10. A
11. O
12. I
13. D
14. K
15. E
16. J
17. P
18. R
19. F
20. T

Day 5 - Classroom Activities

1. An Alternative Ending

Kind of Activity: Creative Writing
Objective: Students will better understand the author's narrative choices by considering alternative endings for the novel.
Common Core State Standards: CCSS.ELA-Literacy.RL.9-10.5
Time: 30 mins

Structure:

Begin by facilitating a general discussion about the novel's final section, particularly the ending itself. Encourage students to discuss what was unexpected, what they liked, how the ending tied together the novel's themes, etc. Move the discussion toward what, if anything, the students would change.

Ask the students to write their own alternative ending for the novel, choosing what they would like to keep about the current ending and what they would change. The piece could take the form of a narrative in the style of the novel, a monologue by Amir (using audio or video equipment if available), or any other format that the instructor deems acceptable.

After the students have had time to write (or record, if applicable), they will share their work with a partner and discuss it. If time permits, ask students to read aloud from their pieces for the entire class, and facilitate a broader discussion.

Ideans for Differentiated Instruction:

-For students who struggle with creative writing, provide examples of alternate endings for them to model their work on.

-Incorporating audiovisual media will help to engage students who struggle with writing but excel at other forms of communication.

Assessment Ideas:

-Have students turn in their alternate endings for evaluation by the instructor.

-Have students comment on one another's pieces using a rubric provided by the instructor. The commentary and rubric can be turned in for evaluation.

2. Authorial Intention

Kind of Activity: Classwide Discussion
Objective: Students will better understand the author's intentions, and begin to consider the importance of authorial intent.
Common Core State Standards: CCSS.ELA-Literacy.RL.9-10.5, CCSS.ELA-Literacy.RL.9-10.6
Time: 20-30 mins

Structure:

Ask the students to make a list of what questions they would ask Khaled Hosseini about *The Kite Runner* if they had the opportunity to interview him. Students should write their questions on slips of paper and place them in a box, from which the instructor will select questions at random. As a class, discuss and attempt to answer these questions based on textual evidence and knowledge of the author's biography.

After this exercise, watch or listen to an interview with Hosseini (see list of links below). Facilitate a class discussion on how their expectations and interpretations compare to Hosseini's explanations. What surprised them about his responses? Did anything he said change their feelings about the novel? Use this as a jumping off point to begin discussing whether authorial intention really matters, or whether stories belong to their readers entirely.

Interviews:

Khaled Hosseini on Fresh Air:
http://www.npr.org/templates/story/story.php?storyId=4795618

Danny Kramer interviews Khaled Hosseini:
http://www.youtube.com/watch?v=56uFHgTs3us

Amazon Interview with Khaled Hosseini:
http://www.amazon.com/gp/mpd/permalink/m3C9HXQTPYW18Y

Ideans for Differentiated Instruction:

-Including video and audio interviews, rather than just textual ones, will allow auditory and visual learners to engage with the material more effectively.

-Pose questions directly to students who may not volunteer, in order to give them a chance to improve their skills.

Assessment Ideas:

-Have the students find and read an interview with Khaled Hosseini and write a brief response paper answering the following question: Has learning about Khaled Hosseini changed your feelings or thoughts about *The Kite Runner*? How?

-Assess students' responses to in-class questions and level of engagement in the class discussion.

Final Paper

Essay Questions

1. How does the novel's ending present the prospect of redemption for Amir?

2. Explore the theme of betrayal in the novel, particularly in light of Amir's relationship with Hassan.

3. Is Hassan a static or dynamic character? How do his qualities help us to better understand Amir as a character? Back up your opinion with evidence from the text.

4. How does the political climate of Afghanistan affect the lives of the characters in the novel?

5. Describe and analyze the father-son relationship between Amir and Baba.

6. How does the adage "History repeats itself" hold true in this novel (both on a political level and among the characters)?

7. Examine the significance of dreams in the novel.

Advice on research sources

A. School or community library

Ask your reference librarian for help locating books on the following subjects:

* Afghanistan

* South Asia

* Ethnic conflict

* Bildungsroman

* Immigration narratives

B. Personal interviews

* Ask people who grew up in a different country and immigrated to the United States what that experience was like.

* Ask people who have been to (or even lived in) Afghanistan about their experiences.

C. Personal experience

Have you ever felt guilty about the way you treated someone? How did that guilt impact your life and decisions? Have you ever had a major family secret suddenly revealed to you? How did that affect your family relationships? Have you ever had to adjust to life in a different country? Have you ever faced prejudice based on your ethnicity?

Grading rubric for essays

Style:

* words: spelling and diction

* sentences: grammar and punctuation

* paragraphs: organization

* essay: structure

* argument: rhetoric, reasonableness, creativity

Content:

* accuracy

* use of evidence

* addresses the question

* completeness

* uses literary concepts

Final Paper Answer Key

Remember that essays about literature should not be graded with a cookie-cutter approach whereby specific words or ideas are required. See the grading rubric above for a variety of criteria to use in assessing answers to the essay questions. This answer key thus functions as a store of ideas for students who need additional guidance in framing their answers.

1. How does the novel's ending present the prospect of redemption for Amir?

   Students should firstly address Amir's need for redemption for his past misdeeds towards Hassan and Ali. There are several ways in which Amir could be seen as achieving redemption. Firstly, he gives Sohrab a new life after his traumatic past in Afghanistan by bringing him to the US and taking him in. Although Amir faces difficulties with the American embassy and is discouraged by the lawyer, he still persists and brings Sohrab to the US. Secondly, he speaks well of Hassan in front of Sohrab, upholding the respect Sohrab has for his father. Lastly, he takes Sohrab kite flying, bringing a semblance of joy to Sohrab's life and allowing him to enjoy being a child. The slight smile that Amir notices on Sohrab's face symbolizes the hope that Sohrab will be able to be happy again. Strong responses will analyze all of these redemptive actions and provide substantiation from the text.

2. Explore the theme of betrayal in the novel, particularly in light of Amir's relationship with Hassan.

   Strong responses will be able to examine several layers of betrayal in the novel. The most obvious example of betrayal is Amir's betrayal of Hassan: he runs away while Hassan is being raped, and frames him for theft in the hopes that Baba will dismiss Hassan and Ali as servants. Students should be able to examine the reasons for these two instances of betrayal (fear in the first, jealousy and guilt in the second) and how one act leads to the other. In addition, strong essays will point out how Amir's betrayal of Hassan mirrors Baba's betrayal of Ali. After fathering a child with Ali's wife, Baba, too, felt guilty and attempted to shower Hassan with attention and affection to alleviate his guilt.

3. Is Hassan a static or dynamic character? How do his qualities help us to better understand Amir as a character? Back up your opinion with evidence from the text.

   Essays should note that Hassan is probably the most consistent character in the novel. As a child, all he wanted was to be a loyal and faithful servant to Amir. Even when Amir betrayed him, Hassan still did not reveal his misdeeds. As an adult, Hassan continues to see himself as Amir faithful friend, but he also knows his place as a Hazara in Afghan society, and as Amir's servant. More nuanced responses would point out that Hassan's character could be read as a foil to Amir's character, especially during their childhood. While we do not really get to know Hassan's adult character very well, we are able to infer from his letters to Amir, and Sohrab's memories, that Hassan was a good father and a guide to Sohrab, providing his son with an education so that he could have a brighter future.

4. How does the political climate of Afghanistan affect the lives of the characters in the novel?

   Students should be able to demonstrate sound knowledge of the political changes in Afghanistan during the time the novel was set--mainly the Russian invasion, the rise of the Taliban, and the fall of the Taliban after the September 11 attacks and American military strikes. Stronger responses should also make links between these political events and the lives of the characters. The Russian invasion inspired a sense of hatred and resentment for many Afghans, like Baba. There was also instability and civil unrest, which made life in Afghanistan difficult. When the Taliban took over, the people initially celebrated, thinking that they would finally have peace. Instead, the Taliban enforced a fundamentalist ideology through violence and fear. Essay responses could address the stoning of the adulterous couple in the novel to illustrate this. Also, Farid warns Amir not to stare at Taliban officials, lest they decide to become aggressive. Although not much is said about the fall of the Taliban, students could refer to how Amir and his wife had given support and assistance to special projects even though they were living in America.

5. Describe and analyze the father-son relationship between Amir and Baba.

   Students should recognize that Amir and Baba's relationship is strained throughout the novel. Amir believes that Baba blames him for his mother's death, and he constantly craving his father's love and attention. Baba also feels detached from Amir because Amir does not fulfill his expectations of strength and masculinity. At times, Baba seems to favor Hassan more. Their relationship does seem to get better superficially after Amir wins the kite tournament, but this is only temporary. It is only after Baba and Amir move to the United States that we are able to see Baba's love for Amir more clearly. Baba wants Amir to be happy in America, despite his own struggles to adapt to the country. Stronger responses will also discuss how Amir and Baba's relationship continues after Baba's death, as Amir learns the truth about Hassan.

6. How does the adage "History repeats itself" hold true in this novel (both on a political level and among the characters)?

Baba's betrayal of Ali (a servant and loyal friend) is repeated when Amir betrays Hassan. Likewise, Hassan's dedication and loyalty are replicated when Amir is kind and dedicated to raising Hassan's son, Sohrab. Strong responses will note that Baba's magnanimity is reflected in Amir's magnanimous act of saving Sohrab. On a political level, Hitler's ethnic cleansing is repeated in the Taliban's massacre of the Hazaras, a connection that is made explicit in the character of Assef, who openly admires Hitler and then joins the Taliban.

7. Examine the significance of dreams in the novel.

   Essays should point out how Hassan's dream about the monster could be a form of foreshadowing, a symbol of the monster that Amir perceives himself to be when he fails to save Hassan and even frames him for theft. The dream that Amir has of Hassan's murder in Chapter 19 could be read as a symbol of Amir's guilt that has been haunting him. In Chapter 23, Amir dreams of Baba merging with him, which could symbolize how alike the two of them are. Amir's fragmented dreams about his past are a manifestation of his subconscious and how he is constantly being plagued by his past.

Final Exam

A. Multiple Choice

Circle the letter corresponding to the best answer.

1. What does Rahim Khan call to ask Amir?

    (A) He asks Amir come see him in Pakistan.
    (B) He asks Amir to clear his name.
    (C) He asks Amir to run a kite for him.
    (D) He asks Amir to buy him groceries.

2. To what does Amir compare his childhood with Hassan?

    (A) A battlefield
    (B) One long and dreary winter
    (C) One long lazy summer day
    (D) A dream

3. What does Hassan say he would rather do than lie to Amir?

    (A) Eat dirt
    (B) Clean the house
    (C) Run away
    (D) Lie to Baba instead

4. Why does Hassan threaten Assef with his slingshot?

    (A) Hassan was just being playful.
    (B) Assef was not a Hazara.
    (C) Assef was about to hit Amir.
    (D) Assef was hitting Hassan.

5. What is the "single greatest moment" of Amir's life when he is 12 years old?

    (A) Writing his first short story
    (B) Joining the Taliban
    (C) Doing well in school
    (D) Seeing his father proud of him

6. What does Amir do after he realizes that Assef is sexually assaulting Hassan?

    (A) He runs away.
    (B) He tries to save Hassan.
    (C) He calls desperately for help.
    (D) He continues to watch until the act was over.

7. Hassan is framed for stealing which of Amir's belongings?

    (A) A book
    (B) A wristwatch
    (C) A bicycle
    (D) A toy

8. Why doesn't Baba want to go back to Peshawar after moving to America?

    (A) He feels that Peshawar was not good for Amir.
    (B) He is afraid of being killed in Peshawar.
    (C) He can amass more wealth in America.
    (D) He leads an easier life in America.

9. What is Soraya's secret?

    (A) She ran away with an Afghan man.
    (B) She betrayed her husband.
    (C) She was infertile.
    (D) She had a child.

10. What illness did Baba suffer from?

    (A) Typhoid
    (B) Cancer
    (C) Heart disease
    (D) Meningitis

11. What book is Soraya reading when Amir first begins to talk to her?

(A) Great Expectations
(B) The Scarlet Letter
(C) Jane Eyre
(D) Wuthering Heights

12. What is Soraya's occupation?

(A) A writer
(B) A seamstress
(C) A teacher
(D) A homemaker

13. How did Rahim Khan get a scar above his eye?

(A) He was fighting with someone at a soccer game.
(B) He fell down and hit his head.
(C) He had accidentally cut himself.
(D) He was struck by a member of the Taliban at a soccer game.

14. How does Ali die?

(A) He has polio.
(B) He is shot by the Taliban.
(C) He is killed by a land mine.
(D) He dies of old age.

15. How did Hassan react to his mother's reappearance?

(A) He embraced her.
(B) He cursed her.
(C) He bolted out of the house.
(D) He welcomed her into his house.

16. What was Baba's true relationship to Hassan?

(A) Baba was Hassan's uncle.
(B) Hassan was Baba's slave.
(C) Baba was Hassan's father.
(D) Baba was Hassan's mentor.

17. Why does Amir leave money under the pillow at Wahid's home?

(A) He believes that it will bring him good luck.
(B) He overhears that Wahid's children would not have enough to eat.
(C) He leaves it there accidentally.
(D) He wants to see if anyone will steal it.

18. What does the beggar on the street tell Amir about his mother?

(A) That she loved Amir very much.
(B) That she was lonely when she was pregnant.
(C) That she is still alive.
(D) That she was more beautiful when she was pregnant.

19. How does Amir get Farid to stop strangling Zaman at the orphanage?

(A) He hits Farid until he is unconscious.
(B) He points out that the children are watching.
(C) He pulls Farid away.
(D) He tries to distract Farid by saying he has found Sohrab.

20. How was the adulterous couple being punished at Ghazi Stadium?

(A) They were being stoned to death.
(B) They were never allowed to see each other again.
(C) They were being sent to jail.
(D) They had to pay a hefty fine.

B. Short Answer

1. How does Amir interpret the infertility that afflicts his marriage?

____

2. Who tracked Soraya down and brought her home after she ran away?

____

3. What medical issue does the General have?

____

4. How does Soraya initially feel about adopting a child?

____

5. What does Amir realize after hearing the eulogies at his father's funeral?

____

6. Why was Farid so enraged with Zaman, the orphanage director?

____

7. Why did Hassan and Farzana agree to move to Kabul with Rahim Khan?

____

8. What is Baba's gift to Amir when he graduates from junior college?

9. What is the doctor's diagnosis about Amir and Soraya's inability to conceive?

10. Why does Amir go back to his old house in Kabul?

C. Vocabulary

Terms		Answers
1. ____	impeccable	A. a pattern made up of many colors, usually tiles
2. ____	clobbering	B. cure
3. ____	stacatto	C. the margins, away from the center
4. ____	taunting	D. a musical term, associated with short and abrupt sounds
5. ____	morose	E. flawless
6. ____	periphery	F. a strong feeling of displeasure borne out of a sense of injustice
7. ____	guileless	G. gloomy
8. ____	indignation	H. having realistic elements mixed with fantasy
9. ____	vigil	I. refuge from harm or danger
10. ____	chagrin	J. doing good for others
11. ____	antidote	K. extreme displeasure
12. ____	permeated	L. hitting violently
13. ____	beneficient	M. innocent, without guise
14. ____	massacred	N. killed on a large scale
15. ____	emaciated	O. thin and weakened
16. ____	oblivion	P. insulting
17. ____	mosaic	Q. sacred quality
18. ____	surreal	R. spread through
19. ____	asylum	S. a state of unawareness
20. ____	sanctity	T. a period of time spent awake, usually in prayer

D. Short Essays

1. Consider the motif of kite-flying in this novel. Why is it important?

2. Analyse the significance of Soraya's role in the novel.

3. How satisfactory do you think the ending of the novel is?

Final Exam Answer Key

A. Multiple Choice Answer Key

1. A
2. C
3. A
4. C
5. D
6. A
7. B
8. A
9. A
10. B
11. D
12. C
13. D
14. C
15. C
16. C
17. B
18. D
19. B
20. A

B. Short Answer Key

1. Amir sees it as a form of retribution for the injustice that he has caused Hassan and Ali to endure.
2. Her father.
3. The General has very bad migraines, during which he locks himself in his room to be alone.
4. She was reluctant, as she always imagined having her own child.
5. Amir realizes that he must step out of his father's shadow and define himself.
6. Zaman was selling children to the Taliban when he was supposed to be protecting them.
7. They wanted to take care of both Rahim Khan and Baba's old house.
8. A car.

9. He diagnoses them as having "unexplained infertility."
10. Amir does not want to forget his past anymore; visiting his old house helps him to confront it.

C. Vocabulary Answer Key

1. E
2. L
3. D
4. P
5. G
6. C
7. M
8. F
9. T
10. K
11. B
12. R
13. J
14. N
15. O
16. S
17. A
18. H
19. I
20. Q

D. Short Essays Answer Key

1. The stronger students would not only consider the literal significance of kite-flying but also definitely consider the symbolic significance. Kite-flying provided a means by which people could bond. Amir and Hassan had bonded over kite-flying and kite-fighting and later on, Amir and Sohrab had bonded over kite-flying as well. Winning the kite-flying competition also symbolized a sense of victory and pride for not only Amir and Hassan but also Baba. When Amir takes Sohrab kite-flying in the last chapter and runs the kite for him, it symbolizes a form of redemption for his past mistakes. Kite-flying provides a sense of liberation and when the Taliban banned kite-flying, they were taking away one of the joys of the

people, which underscores their inhumane nature of ruling the country.

2. The stronger students will firstly point out how Soraya had played a consistent supportive role in Amir's life and also made him a better person by causing him to reflect on what it means to love another person as well as to have the courage to confess one's past transgressions and to tell the truth. They would also analyze Soraya's maternal role in embracing Sohrab as her own child and also to compensate for her lack of ability to have her own. More nuanced answers would also note how she becomes the voice in the novel who speaks up against the discrimination of women in the patriarchal Afghan society.
3. There are several ways to approach this question. Students could argue that it is indeed satisfactory because it is realistic. It does not have a "happy-ever-after" ending but it does acknowledge that the road to redemption is not easy. They could also argue that it is satisfactory because it presents hope for both Amir and Sohrab to leave their past behind and have a chance at happiness. Alternatively, students could also argue that it is rather unsatisfactory because it leaves a lot of unresolved issues and unanswered questions. We never really get to know what happens to Sohrab eventually and whether or not he will be safe and happy in America with Soraya and Amir.

32880064R00082

Made in the USA
Middletown, DE
08 January 2019